RISE

The 8 Keys to Overcoming Adversity
and Living a Life You'll Love

KWESI MILLINGTON

DEDICATION

FOR MY TWO "C"s

For my mother, Carolyn

Your love, compassion, patience and wisdom are endless gifts to me, and I finally am starting to live a life that is living up to what you have tried to instill in me. The man I am and am becoming would never have been possible without you. I love you.

For my beautiful wife, Cindy

I have heard that success is a process, but it starts with a single moment – a single decision. I made a decision when I met you. I decided that the person that I was – in life, in relationships, in general – was no longer acceptable. I had to be better. I had to be more. For you. You are my strength, my unwavering support, and the better part of my soul. I love you!

CONTENTS

INTRODUCTION

From October 14, 2007 to the writing of this book, I feel like I have lived many lives. This book is about those lives, my story.

However...*my* story is *your* story.

The questions that I've had to answer in my journey to where I am now are the *same* questions that you have to answer in your life. This book is simply my answers to these questions. These are the eight keys that I have used to unlock the code to getting through the struggles and setbacks that we all inevitably go through.

Pastor T.D. Jakes says, "Our struggles are similar; it's our solutions that differ." I truly believe that. From sharing my story with others, I have found that we all go through pain in life. I used to measure how much pain someone else has been through with my own, as if there is some kind of "struggle scale." Yes, there are some pains that may be greater than others. However, I have seen third-degree burn victims handle their adversity better than sprained wrist victims. I have seen cancer patients handle their diagnoses better than cold and flu patients. It truly is *not* what happens to you, as W. Mitchell says, but what you do about it.

Life is all about learning. Here is what I've learned in life, from both experiencing, and reading. Experience is the best teacher, but not the only one. Through my story, my wish is that you find *yours*. Through my mental struggles, may you reach your *own* solutions. My prayer for you is: whatever you are going through, I hope that with my words, you may find *your* wisdom. Notice I said "find." It's already there. The answers are *already* inside of you. You just may need some prompting to bring it out. Let's begin the journey – the journey to find your answers, your wisdom.

It's time to rise.

1 ASSOCIATION

The modern study of chaos began with the creeping realization in the 1960s that quite simple mathematical equations could model systems every bit as violent as a waterfall. .... In weather, for example, this translates into what is only half-jokingly known as the Butterfly Effect—the notion that a butterfly stirring the air today in Peking can transform storm systems next month in New York.

- James Gleick

LEAKS IN YOUR HOSE

When I was younger, I regularly visited my aunt's home in Washington, D.C. I didn't live in a large home, so when my mother would send me from my home in Toronto, Canada, to the U.S. for the summer, I always had a great time. My aunt simply added me to the family, and I became the fourth child, along with my three cousins. Whatever she got them involved in, I was involved in. She enrolled me in soccer camp and Bible camp. She packed me into the car and we lived on McDonald's hamburgers as we made our way to Busch Gardens. I had so much fun, and made so many memories. Even staying around the house, although rare, was fun.

And what kid does not like playing in the backyard? Specifically, playing with the garden hose? When one of my cousins was holding the front of the hose, spraying everything (and everyone) they could find, the solution was always to fold the hose at some point, to stop the water flow. This works every time. However, eventually, the hose will wear out in various areas, from the folding solution, as well as general wear and tear. Holes develop. You tape them up. Holes develop at another point. You tape those up too. However, eventually there will be too much tape, too many holes, and then it will be time.

You'll have to buy a new hose.

LIFE LESSON

When I became a police officer in 2005, I thought life was great. I had held a series of low-paying go-nowhere jobs. I didn't really have a lot of direction when I went to school. I graduated from Ryerson University in 2000 with a Bachelor of Commerce Degree. Sounds nice – I have a "B.Comm." degree! I really just had what I call a "Diet Degree."

What's a "Diet Degree"? Well, sometimes people try one diet in order to lose weight, they give up, then try another – all in futility. They may try the "low carb" diet for a while, then the "juice diet," then the "low fat" diet. At the end, they are just left with a mess of attempts with no results. When I was in school, I tried programming courses, then I switched to marketing courses, added some finance courses, and ended up with enough credits to graduate, but no direction.

I'm sure you've heard the quote: "If you don't know where you're going, any road will get you there." I think it should be: "If you don't know where you're going, *no road will get you there.*" Without direction, you wander. Not to your destination, but to some unknown place. A place that leads you to ask, "How did I get here?"

HOW DID I GET HERE?

When someone gives you something in life, often we think it is prestigious if other people tell us it is. We add value to something because we perceive that other people give it value, without questioning if we ourselves think it is worth having.

I graduated as an RCMP (Royal Canadian Mounted Police) Officer on May 16, 2005. I'm not saying that wasn't a great accomplishment. I'm not saying that I wasn't proud. I'm not saying that I didn't hold the career in high regard. I did. But I never asked myself: "Is this what I *really* want to do with my life?" Most people don't.

Regardless, I jumped in. My first four months were rough, due mostly to my militant training officer, but also because of my own insecurities and inability (or unwillingness) to stand up for myself. However, I got through my training period (six months total), and started to love my job. And myself. Too much. I let the uniform go to my head. Not *on* the job, but *off* it.

I gave everything to the job. I stood up at work for the principles promoted by the Force (the RCMP). HIPCAR was the acronym: Honesty, Integrity, Professionalism, Compassion, Accountability, Respect.
However, in my personal life, I wasn't the same.

Remember the holes in that garden hose? Well, in life, if you are exhibiting traits in *one* area, you must do it in *all* areas of your life, or holes will appear. If you are honest with co-workers, you need to be honest with friends. If you have compassion for those you know, then you need to have compassion for those you don't. If you respect some, you must respect all (or at least their right to be who they are).

I didn't realize it then, but I was on a crash trajectory for October 14, 2007, and all of the events following that date. Not because of who I was *on* the job, but because of who I became *off* it.

CREATING THE LEAK

I got married for the first time in January 2006 to a wonderful woman. Who I wasn't ready for. I realize that I am not the first person who has ever married someone even while doubting the entire decision. I just never thought I would actually be one of those who would do it. But I did.

I know now that I wasn't ready to live with anyone yet.
I know now that I wasn't ready to be engaged.
I know now that I wasn't ready to get married.

And if I was to look back honestly, I can say that I knew it *then* too.

But I took the cowardly way out. I stayed quiet. I did what I thought I was supposed to do. I got married. I tried to pretend that I was happy. I tried to convince myself that I was in the right situation and in the right place. I shouldn't say convince. I should really say I ignored a lot of things.

I ignored that I wasn't happy in my relationship.
I ignored that I wasn't in the right situation.
I ignored the fact that bringing other women into your life when you're married is wrong.

Life is about decisions. When you *decide* you are going to be successful, you will be presented with opportunities to be successful. In the same way, when you decide that you will allow infidelity into your life, you will be presented with opportunities to be unfaithful. Life is all about decisions.

I decided, instead of just walking away from a marriage that was wrong, to be unfaithful to my marriage vows. I know now that taking that course of action will always lead to ruin. I knew it then. But I made a *decision* to ignore that fact.

In May of 2007, my marriage came to an end. No surprise there. The problem is that I did not change the way that I acted towards women. I dated and dumped as if there's a prize for the pursuit of multiple women.

I lied in my personal life, thinking that all of the areas of my life were in their own compartments. However, just like a rock thrown in water causes ripples in other previously calm areas, so, too, did the imbalance in one area of my life cause problems in another.

It's all related.

OCTOBER 14, 2007

There are few careers where "Lunch Time" can be at 1 AM in the morning. Policing is one of them. When the call came in that would forever change my life, I thought I was in a good place. I had a career I loved, in a unit that was much quieter than the busy city. I liked that. I wasn't an "action junkie" cop. When the high speed chase was on, I went for backup out of duty, not desire. The call that many police officers hate – the family dispute "counsellor" call – was the one I used to love. I come from a single parent family, and I get a huge sense of satisfaction in trying to bring disputing loved ones together. I don't want others to have to go through the same hardships that I did as a result of being in a separated family.

That's why when years later a lawyer looked right at me in court and said, "I bet you couldn't wait to use your Taser, could you?", I had to laugh inside. I was thinking, "If you only knew me! If you only knew that I was a victim of bullying in my youth." Those types of statements are alien to who I am.

In the early morning hours of October 14, 2007, I and three other officers received a dispatch call to respond to a man causing a disturbance inside of the international terminal of Vancouver International Airport. A man, later identified as Robert Dziekanski, was reported throwing luggage around an airport. Four police officers showed up, one used a Taser (that's me), and Dziekanski was placed under arrest. Minutes later, his heart stopped. There is no absolute proof as to the cause of death, and the opinions vary.

Some people accuse me of electrifying him to death with my Taser. That's an opinion.

Some people accuse the four of us of using excessive force, which caused him to die. That's an opinion. Some people, including some doctors, say that he had a pre-existing medical condition based on his profuse sweating and agitation when we encountered him, and that as soon as he was arrested, regardless of method, he was likely to die. That is also just an opinion.

There are many *opinions* about what happened that night, but here are the *facts*. Robert Dziekanski (hereafter referred to as "the man") arrived on a flight from Poland to be picked up by his mother. For reasons unknown, he started to damage airport property, including attempted destruction of electronics and furniture. At that point, we (three other officers and I) were called to intervene. After seeing the man on the secure side of the airport terminal, we attempted to communicate with him. The language barrier prevented proper communication; the man picked up and opened a stapler, and started to advance towards us. I pulled out and used my Taser, and we handcuffed and arrested him. He started to go into cardiac arrest soon after. Despite firemen and ambulance attendant intervention, he died.

In police training we learn that when police officers have to intervene, tragedy can result. However, just like a death in the family, you are never prepared when it happens to you. I knew we had to apprehend and restrain the man that night, but I never thought in a million years that he would die. And although I was told that bad things could happen in our job, and though I was reassured that any other officer in my place would have acted the same way, I can't help but think about the events of that night, and wonder if it could have ended differently.

When a situation moves quickly, it's tempting to analyze and play out imaginary alternate endings afterwards. I had only one reality. The truth.

The *truth* is that we did our jobs. A tragedy resulted, but we did what we were trained to do.

The *truth* is that the events of that night were recorded and we (the four officers) knew that the video was made. I knew it even before I gave my statement.

The *truth* is that we all gave statements outlining what happened that night.

The *truth* is that a report was given by an RCMP officer on national television outlining the events, without anyone contacting us or reviewing our statements beforehand.

The *truth* is that when the public saw the video after hearing the incorrect reporting of the events, there was an outcry for something to be done about "the cover up."

The *truth* is that there was a public inquiry into the events of that night in October. I testified on March 2-4, 2009, and I was looking forward to finally getting my side of the story out and achieving vindication.

The *truth* is that the judge overseeing the inquiry wrote a scathing report afterwards, accusing us (the four officers involved) of many things, most notably of exaggerating our statements in October in order to make Mr. Dziekanski's actions appear worse than they were and our actions appear justified.

The *truth* is that I had previously been cleared of any wrongdoing by the crown prosecutors in British Columbia, Canada, as well as by the RCMP, and was quite transparent with my statements and testimony at the inquiry.

The *truth* is that for whatever reason, a special prosecutor was subsequently allowed to review the details of the case, and was given carte blanche to charge any or all of us with a criminal offence. This—despite the clearing of our names previously.

The *truth* was that in 2011, I was charged with perjury (lying under oath with intent to mislead), for statements made at the public inquiry. An inquiry that I later found out was not mandatory but that I chose to participate in.

THE AFTERMATH

At the time of the writing of this chapter, I stood convicted of perjury. I was convicted in February 2015 and sentenced to 30 months' imprisonment in June 2015. I appealed the conviction in June 2016 in the Appeal Court of British Columbia, Canada. In July 2016 my appeal was rejected.

But...life must go on.

THE LESSON

Life is all about lessons. Lessons that will be thrown at you repeatedly until you learn them.

Do you keep getting into bad relationships over and over again? Look deeper. There's a lesson about yourself that you *must* learn before you get the partner you want.

Do you keep ending up in jobs that don't fulfill you? Look deeper. There's a lesson to learn there.

Recurrent patterns happening in your life are meant to teach you some lesson. Learning that lesson is imperative. Like that garden hose, the "leaks" will continue to happen in your life until you learn to stop the source of the water.

I believe that I was meant to be at that airport on that tragic night. On the job, I was humble, but in my personal life I was not. The leaky hose from my aunt's backyard was my life. My *entire* life has been utterly derailed by the occupational crash that started on October 14, 2007. I have been accused of murdering a man with excessive force. I have been charged with a crime I did not commit.

Charged with perjury – lying to a judge under oath. On February 20, 2015, I was convicted of that crime, and on June 22, 2015, I was hauled off to a jail cell for something I never did.

The entire process brought out the worst in courtroom spectators, news story commenters, and a barrage of online haters. My ancestry has been degraded by people who choose the lowest common denominator response of hate. They have called me "nigger" more times than I choose to count. Not to mention comments that I've received through email calling me "a fucking black prick," "a murdering motherfucker," "a lying piece of shit," "a corrupt cop that I'd like to see die" and many more that my subconscious mind has mercifully blocked out.

I believe there are many lessons that this was all meant to teach me. I'll get into more of them later on, but one of the main lessons I've learned is what I call "Holistic Humility." If you're humble in one area of your life, you must be humble in all areas.

On the job, I was humble. Outside, I wasn't. It's that simple. I don't think I was aware of that at the time, but looking back, it is now obvious.

Contrast that to now. I strive to be humble in every way, every day.

KEY QUESTIONS TO ASK YOURSELF

Look at your life. Is there an area where you exhibit excellence? Is there another area that you have let slide?

Look at your personality. Are *you* humble in one area, but not in another? Are you trustworthy to some people and not to others? Is lying acceptable to you in some circumstances and not in others? Remember that life is holistic. What you are in one area, you need to be in all areas.

If you forget this, don't worry: Life has a special way of reminding you. The reminders may be small at first – if you're lucky. Know, however, that the reminders may be drastic. Self-examination is a lot easier.

Ask yourself: Am I holistic in the areas of my life?

INTRODUCING: THE 1%

Forget giving 100%. Just give 1%.

Author James Altucher described this idea in his book, *The Choose Yourself Guide to Wealth*. The concept is so powerful that it applies to more than household finances. Making small improvements in the various areas of your life will, over time, make a huge impact. There is power in habits. Habits are simply small steps done repeatedly over time. A 1% improvement in various areas of your life will lead to a 100% change over time.

According to this principle, in each section you will find a "1% Worksheet" that will give you a guide to help you improve in each of the eight keys to ascending above adversity. Take the time to work through them. The questions are not difficult – they are meant to help you to apply what you have read. Psychological studies show that when you read, you have a chance of changing your behaviour. However, when you apply what you've read, you are much more likely to change your behaviour.

That being said, let's get to your first Worksheet.

YOUR 1% WORKSHEET – ASSOCIATION

Think about 2-3 major difficult situations that you have gone through in your life. Is there one area of your life that may have been "off" leading to those situations? Journal your thoughts.

On a scale of 1-10, rate yourself in the following areas:

1.   Finances:
2.   Personal Health:
3.   Emotional & Spiritual Health:
4.   Family & Spousal Relationships:
5.   Friends & Acquaintances Relationships:

Now suggest a way that you can improve, even by 1%, in all of the above relationships (if you rated any a 10, list a way that you can help someone else improve in that area by 1%):

1.   Finances:

2.   Personal Health:

3.   Emotional & Spiritual Health:

4.   Family & Spousal Relationships:

5.   Friends & Acquaintances Relationships:

2 ANGLE

Everything we hear is an opinion, not a fact. Everything we see is a perspective, not the truth.

- Marcus Aurelius

WERE WE AT THE SAME MOVIE?

Have you ever been to a movie with someone, and come out with completely different opinions about it? I have walked into movies that have gotten high ratings, rave reviews by critics, and the craved "Oscar buzz." I can remember walking out of movies thinking "What was all the fuss about?" Conversely, I have watched movies that have been poorly received and thoroughly enjoyed them.

We all have different opinions and views. You may see something differently than I see it. We colour the world through our own life experiences. That is natural. But sometimes we need to step back. It is not a big deal to look at a Hollywood movie with only your own opinions. But in life, we need to be able to see situations from the point of view of others. If we do not, there can be trouble.

HOW I SAW IT IN 2009

In January 2009, a public inquiry began that looked into the use of Tasers in policing, as well as the death of Robert Dziekanski at Vancouver Airport. The reasons for the public inquiry are open for debate; however I was clear about what I thought about testifying at this televised inquiry.

I was excited and hopeful. Nervous, yes. However, my thoughts were that I would be able to "clear my name" if you will.

Before this point, I had been cleared of any wrongdoing by my own police force, and two other police departments. I was found to be acting within the scope of my duties and was still employed by my own police force, the RCMP.

However, the fact that the original incident was incorrectly reported by an RCMP representative left a lasting impression in the public eye that there was some type of cover-up. There was an incorrect assumption that there was some conspiracy to hide facts from the general public. This is despite the fact that the entire incident was recorded (a fact known to the four officers involved) and that there were many live witnesses to the actual incident on the night of October 14, 2007. Nevertheless, there was a widespread opinion of police corruption as the "Braidwood Inquiry" of 2009 began.

Going into the Braidwood Inquiry, I saw testifying as a chance to clear the air. I saw it as an opportunity to tell my side of the story. My thought and hope was that taking the stand in March 2009 would give the presiding judge and the public the view of an officer that wasn't just a uniform, but was also a human being. Someone who had done his best in the situation presented. Someone who did the job he was trained to do, even though tragedy resulted. Someone who told the truth, the whole truth, and nothing but the truth.

The judge, many of the lawyers, and much of the public chose not to see that.

My father always used to tell me "the truth is what you believe." With everything in life, the truth that *you* choose to believe will be the truth that you will live by. It may or may not be the real truth, but for all intents and purposes, it will be the truth for you. Your actions will follow from the truths that *you* believe.

HOW DID THE PUBLIC SEE IT?

The presiding view in Vancouver in 2009 was that a confused, distraught middle-aged man was just trying to be reunited with his mother after a long flight from his homeland of Poland. The general opinion was that he ran into the big, bad cops, they roughed him up, and one of them electrocuted the poor man to death.

And no testimony from *any* police officer, no matter how logical, was going to change that view. In my naiveté, I thought perhaps my testimony would have. I couldn't have been more wrong. And I *should* have known it going in.

An inquiry is not like a normal court case. In a typical courtroom, you have a prosecution team and a defence team. The "accused" either chooses to testify or not. Should testifying be chosen, the defence lawyer asks questions in order to demonstrate the client's innocence. The prosecution lawyer asks questions and makes statements to attempt to prove to the judge or jury that the accused is guilty. From the accused person's perspective, there is a reasonable expectation of a "friendly" line of questioning from the defence lawyer, and a more accusatory or criticizing tone from the prosecution.

However, the Braidwood Inquiry worked more like an open mic night at a comedy club.

Anyone with "interests" seemed to be able to attend and ask their questions. There were lawyers, a civil liberties representative – even a representative from Taser International – who were allowed to ask questions. (In 2017, Taser International changed its name to Axon Enterprise, Inc., with the mission stated on its home page to "protect life.") Despite the two and a half days of my testimony in March of 2009 and questioning from numerous angles, I was okay with all of that. Yes, I was surprised at all of the various interests that were represented. Yes, I was surprised that the first line of questioning – from someone who was supposed to be a neutral lawyer – was accusatory and had the obvious goal of derision and embarrassment. Yes, I was surprised that the judge seemed to have his mind made up that I and the other officers were guilty of *something* before we finished speaking. Yet, still I had hope that the public would see that we acted in accordance with our training and did the best we could despite the chaotic circumstances.

FEELINGS OVER FACTS

People may not always remember what you say, but they will always remember how you made them feel.

- Maya Angelou

In the world of public speaking, they say that what the audience *feels* is more important than what the audience *hears.* I did not realize it at the time, but what I had to say in that inquiry would never have mattered to the presiding judge, a few lawyers in that court, and some of the public.

They *felt* that Robert Dziekanski was a victim.
They *felt* sadness for his mother.
They *felt* that what the four officers did was excessive and/or wrong.

In life, what people feel will always trump what they hear. Feelings are powerful. We often justify decisions with logic – but make them with our emotions. Feelings often win over facts.

SPINNING STORIES

You can't connect the dots looking forward. You can only connect them looking back.

- Steve Jobs

After the inquiry was completed, the Braidwood Report was an affront. I read his opinion that we – the officers involved – lied on our statements and reports to make it appear as though Dziekanski was more aggressive than he was in order to minimize our actions. Actions that we were *justified* to take. Actions that had resulted in us being *cleared* of any wrongdoing by at least three separate Police Forces. Actions that we were *trained* to take.

The report angered me. However, I read it and put it away, thinking the saga was over.

It wasn't. And looking back, I now believe that the report was written with the intention that it be used to support the charges of perjury that were laid against us in 2011.

That's my view. That's the movie I saw. Of course, I could be wrong, but hey, it's a *feeling*.

ENGLISH VS MATH CLASS

In school, I always did better in English classes than in Math classes. In English, there are many ways to look at things. Many ways to interpret the Shakespearean play we were reading. Many ways to approach any topic. In Math class, however, there is only one solution to each problem.

Life works like an English class. There are many angles at which to approach something. People will look at different situations in different ways. They will see them from different angles. Your angle isn't wrong, nor is mine. It is just the way that we interpret the same movie.

Understanding this has helped me to view the Braidwood Inquiry and Braidwood Report differently. Understanding this has helped me understand why I was charged and convicted of perjury, and sentenced to 30 months in jail. In life, we try so hard to change people's angles of situations. However, the only way to do that is if *they* are open to it. Trying to change someone else's angle, if they are not open to it, is like trying to pour water into an overflowing glass. You won't be able to get more water into it, no matter how hard you try.

YOUR MOVIE

In your life, what movie are you watching? Is someone trying to change your angle on something? Are you trying to change someone else's? An old saying advises us to seek first to *understand*, then to be *understood*. When approaching a situation where a person sees something from a different angle, look at trying to comprehend them rather than to change them.

Have they gone through a situation that would cause them to have their view?

Do they have different background experiences that would make their angle different from yours?

Are you getting your back up just because someone does not back you up?

Remember that people live in their own clouds in life. They have gone through their own ups and downs. By the time your paths cross, they have lived an *entirely* different movie than you have. What may seem obvious to you may not be obvious to them. What may seem like "common sense" to them may be totally foreign to you. Simply understanding that people are watching their own movies and may therefore write different endings will ease your soul and change your life.

YOUR 1% WORKSHEET – ANGLE

1.   Think back to a time in your life when you were "wronged." Was it a relationship that ended? A job that you were let go from? A business partner or friend who did something that you did not approve of? Write out a "script" from the other person's point of view. Write it in first person as if you are the other person. What would they see? Even if it feels wrong to you, write out what they might have seen completely from their viewpoint.

2.   Look over what you have written. Was there any part of the angle of the situation that you may not have seen when you originally experienced it? (Hindsight is 20/20 after all). Journal your thoughts.

3.   The next time that you are in a situation where you feel you have been treated unfairly, go through this exercise again. You may find that the other person was completely wrong, but at least you will strengthen your "empathy muscle" and start to look at situations more neutrally.

3 ACCOUNTABILITY

You pass from childhood to adulthood when you take full responsibility for your life.

- Jim Rohn

MOM & DAD

I grew up in a single-parent home. Kind of. I was born in Montreal, Canada, and around the age of five, my father decided to leave Canada – and me – and fly back to his home country of Trinidad. My mother and I moved to Toronto, and that is where I have lived for most of my life.

I say "kind of" because my father didn't completely disappear. He sent money to my mother to help take care of me. But more than that, at various times in my youth, I packed my bags and spent the summer in Trinidad with him, and my brother Kojo. (Eventually we would be joined by my sister Nia, and later, my brother Kwende.)

Compared to the average boy who is raised in a single-parent home, I spent more time with my father, and for that I am grateful. However, it is *not* the same as having your father present in your life at all times. I learned that while growing up with my best friend Ian. Ian had his father in his life completely – the way a father is supposed to be in a child's life. Ian's dad spent time with him. He coached him on the soccer field. He helped him with his homework. Looking back, it is obvious to me now that I was very jealous. I longed for that constant father-son companionship. I wondered why I did not have that in my life. I thought about asking my father why he left. But I never did.

We spent our summers together, one Christmas in Trinidad, and even the last summer when my father visited me in Toronto before his death on August 29, 1996. During all the time together, the one question that I never asked my father was: "Dad, why did you leave?"

THE BLAME GAME

The easiest thing in life to do is to look for a scapegoat for your shortcomings. My easy go-to was "I didn't have a father in my life." When I failed in anything, I would look to see if the person who succeeded lived in a two-parent home. If they did, I would say to myself, "See! That's why they are confident and successful; they have *both* parents!" Of course I saw numerous single-parent success stories, but doesn't it seem as if we focus all too often on what we *do not* have?

I have a strong mother, I had an occasionally present father, and I live in one of the best countries in the world, yet I kept focusing on what I didn't have. Worse yet, I justified anything I couldn't do, or anything that didn't work, through a faulty set of "life lenses."

That faulty thinking came through in many areas, most specifically, in my relationships. The danger in feeling like a victim of circumstance is that you fail to take accountability for your life. When you fail to take accountability, you are doomed to repeat and re-live the negative things that occur in your life. In my relationships with women, I would always cut them short, citing one reason or another. The truth is, I would see difficulty as a reason to leave, not as an opportunity to grow, learn, and fix the problem.

It always comes down to one battle: the external vs. the internal.

If you believe the external events in your life affect what you can and cannot do, then that will be the reality that plays out in your life. When you understand that your internal response determines your success or failure, that changes everything. Holocaust survivor Viktor Frankl said it best: we have the ability "to choose one's attitude in any given set of circumstances, to choose one's own way."

It took me a long time to learn this.

IT'S THEIR FAULT

In 2007, I showed up to a call that required a physical response. At the end of the altercation, a man died. The incident was misreported, creating an allegation that there was some type of cover-up.

I blamed the RCMP for sending a representative to speak *for* us, without ever speaking first *to* us. "It's *their* fault." I said.

In 2009, I attended and testified at an inquiry and was asked to explain my role in the call from October 2007. I told the truth, but at the end of the inquiry, the presiding judge wrote a report that accused me and the other three officers of lying in our post-incident statements, and in his courtroom. This led to the appointment of a special prosecutor and subsequently a charge of perjury in 2011.

Let the Blame Game begin.

I blamed the judge for being biased.

I blamed the RCMP for not releasing a statement in our defence.

I blamed the province of British Columbia, thinking that the reason I was charged is because of the bias that the general population had against the police – which put pressure on the powers that be to charge us.

I looked for anyone to blame for the situation I was in. And blaming others feels good. It's like that glass of scotch after a hard day's work. It feels good at the time – yet it really does you no good in the long run. Yet I held on to that way of looking at the case – and my life in general – until changes in another area of my life caused me to look at everything *much* differently.

THE TURNING POINT

I have never been great at relationships. By the end of 2012, I had several ex-girlfriends, an ex-wife, and an ex-fiancée. I could take the easy road. I could say that I never had a great example of a good relationship because I grew up in a single-parent home. I could say that my father had five children with five different women, and I followed that example of "spouse swapping." I could say a lot of things.

But that would be falling into the Blame Game yet again.

The truth is, I never really considered what a vow and a promise was in relationships. I did not set any standards for myself, and therefore I had no direction as to what I would or would not do in a relationship. As with sailing, if you don't set your sails in a specific direction, you will never get anywhere. You have to decide what you're going to do – and *not* do – in order to have any chance to succeed.

For some reason, meeting my wife Cindy changed all of that for me. In life, everything comes down to a decision. When I met Cindy, as simple as it may sound, I did just that – I made a decision. Well, actually I made a few decisions.

I decided that I would not be the reason for anyone else's heartbreak anymore.

I decided that I would never lie to the woman I was with ever again.

I decided that I would do anything I needed to in order to be a worthy partner in a relationship.

Finally, I decided that I would take ownership for anything that ever went wrong or needed fixing in my relationships from that day forward.

It's not easy. But it's the best decision I ever made. I just didn't know how far-reaching that positive decision would be.

THE BURDEN AND THE BLESSING

When you take ownership in your life – truly take ownership – everything changes. Your life goes from chance to change. Your decisions change. Your thoughts change. Your actions change.

The truth is a blessing...and a burden.

Once you decide to take ownership for something, it's like home ownership vs. renting. When you rent a home, it's easy. When the fridge breaks down, you call the landlord. When there's a leak, it's someone else's responsibility. When money needs to be spent, someone *else* has to spend it.

However, when you *own* a home, everything is on *you.* The burden of renovations, repair and expenses falls on you. You chose to own the home, so you have to fix it. However, within that burden also comes the blessing. Some of the monthly money you pay goes toward mortgage costs, but some of it goes toward the principal— the actual cost of the house. The money you pay for renovations or repair goes into building your equity as opposed to someone else's. You get to choose how to make your home look exactly the way you want it – no rules. There is a freedom in ownership.

There is a freedom in ownership, despite the hardship. That statement applies to your life as well.

When I decided to own who I was in my relationship with Cindy, that decision mushroomed to all areas of my life. I finally realized that I had to own everything. No matter how hard it may be.

I had to own that I decided to become a police officer. It really doesn't matter who or what also contributed to the 2007 call, the 2009 inquiry, the 2011 charge and the 2015 conviction. The point is that I decided to sign the paperwork on May 16, 2005, to become a police officer with the Royal Canadian Mounted Police.

Everything in life goes back to a decision that I decided to make.

I also had to own that, even though he took actions that created the necessity for intervention, my actions contributed to the death of another human being. Being told that I acted appropriately and perfectly within the scope of my training alleviates me from any wrongdoing on paper, but it does not take away from the daily second guessing that I have gone through from that night forward. Could I have tried something else? Would the result have changed if a different device (other than the Taser) had been used?

The burden of ownership can, however, become a blessing.

Sleepless nights. Prescription drugs. Thoughts of suicide. A diagnosis of depression and PTSD in 2010. All of these became part of my life over the next few years. But I've learned that feeling of despair can be alleviated through ownership.

Just as owning my actions in a relationship has changed my life, so has owning my actions following being charged and falsely convicted done the same.

THE CURE FOR DEPRESSION

As I write this, I have just learned that June 26 is the UN International Day Against Drug Abuse. That day brings awareness to the international goal of creating a society free of drug abuse.

I understand the fight. But here is the fight that really needs to happen. The war need not be against drugs. The *real* war should be against despair.

Despair comes from the Latin word "desperare" meaning "down" (de) and "to hope" (sperare). When your hope is down, you feel pain. When you feel that pain, you want to numb it. Whether it's through drugs, sex, alcohol, or mindless activity, you want to numb the pain. For every drug I've ever taken in my life, although I likely convinced myself at the time that it was to make me feel better, it was actually taken to stop me from feeling. It was taken because my hope was 'down'.

Two specific days changed the way I feel about myself and my future.

The first was in 2011. I was sitting at the edge of my bed with a thought. In my hands were the blue sleeping pills that my doctor prescribed for me. I wondered: "How many?" "How many of these would I need to take...?" That wasn't because I wanted to feel better. That was because I wanted *not* to feel. That was a feeling of despair.

I truly believe that the only thing stopping me that day was a feeling of responsibility to others. I was in a relationship, and I had a mother who was aging and whose finances I was taking care of. I got up off the bed and had another thought. "Is there anyone else I can help?"

I believe that thought was sent to me. I believe that I was supposed to walk into a gym that I never heard of before just a few days later. I believe that I was led to dust off my Personal Training Specialist certification and to start helping people again. I believe that train of divinely inspired thoughts saved my life.

I truly believe that the cure for depression is not drugs. The cure is helping someone else. The cure is finding someone that you can help, and giving to others in some way.

For me that was personal training and health coaching in 2011. That was volunteering with food banks and youth in 2012. And I did not know it at the time, but it was also an important day in June of 2013.

THE SECOND DAY

The second day that changed my life was the day that I walked into a Toastmasters meeting. To be precise, it was the *second* day that I walked into a Toastmasters meeting. Toastmasters is an organization that helps people all over the world develop confidence, as well as leadership and public speaking skills.

The reason that I say that the second meeting made a difference, is because I met a woman at my second meeting that told me about a different club. Sometimes – actually, all times – you need to listen to your intuition. Something inside told me, "Kwesi, this first group isn't the right fit for you. This woman has energy. Go see what her group has to offer that might be different." I followed that voice, and it was one of the best decisions that I have ever made.

What is *your* second day? I believe that if you hate the job that you're in, the relationship that you have settled for, or anything else in your life, you *need* to change it. Listen to the voice inside that demands more from you. If you do – if you make that change – getting rid of the situations and people that are bringing you down will start a new day for you. *your* second day. Wake up anew and enjoy your life.

My "Second Day" was starting my Toastmasters journey with my new group. It sounds simple enough. Participate in an impromptu speaking session called "Table

Topics." Sign up for a few 5 to 7 minute speeches and tell some stories from your life.

Wrong. *Not* simple. I was terrified. It took me almost a month to participate in Table Topics and four months to sign up and deliver my first speech, the "icebreaker," in which I had to introduce myself and my life journey thus far to the club. But I did it. And I discovered that sometimes God pushes some buttons inside of you when you're doing what you are supposed to do.

That button was pressed. After I spoke, I got back into my car and turned on a YouTube video from a man by the name of Les Brown. He said something that I have never forgotten. He said: "You have greatness within you." He wasn't talking directly to me, of course, but he may as well have been. He went on to say that we all have something inside of us that we need to do, and if we don't do it, no one else will. Les Brown made me realize that words can change people's lives. I then had a crazy thought: "What if I could change people's lives through *my* words?"

MESSAGE FROM THE MOON

Do you remember learning how moonlight is created?

The moon creates no light on its own. It reflects the light from the sun, and that is how you see what you know as "moonlight." In essence, the moon *borrows* its light from the sun, in order to produce light. Sometimes *we* have to borrow someone else's light, to help ours shine bright.

Sometimes *we* have to borrow someone else's light, to help ours shine bright.

Remember that woman who led me to the second meeting? When I wasn't sure about speaking, she nudged me into joining Toastmasters. When I didn't know who to turn to in order to improve, she nudged me in the direction of world class speakers in order to solidify my skills. I love to speak now, and I owe a lot of that to the little nudges that my friend gave me along the way.

Are you trying to do everything yourself? Are you too stubborn to believe that you need someone else's light from time to time to help you shine? Don't be afraid to ask for help. Asking doesn't make you weak; it helps you to remain strong.

The ability to write is a gift I have been given. I have been writing my whole life, and had my first published poem when I was five years old. However, it is the ability to lift those words off the page and to share them through speaking that has been the real gift. The opportunity to change lives through the words I have written and spoken is a true blessing. I am eternally grateful to my friend for her kind words, to Toastmasters for starting me on that journey, and to Les Brown for being my "surrogate virtual father" when I desperately needed guidance.

Discovering and learning the art of Speaking has transformed my life, and has helped me to help others transform theirs.

But there's more...

PAYING THE DEBT

I don't know what you believe. I believe that there is something above us and in us. Call it God. Call it Infinite Intelligence. Call it whatever you want. I believe that God lives inside of us, and the answers to everything we need are given to us if we only dare to ask. "Ask and it shall be given." That's what the verse says, and I believe it.

I have asked repeatedly, "What is the best use of my life?" and "What direction should I be heading in?" And here is what I believe...

I believe that we all have a debt to pay. There is good and bad out there, and we have an accountability to do as much for others as we can before we die. If it involves giving to others and service to others, do it. Find something in your life that improves the lives of others. Whether on the job or not, you should find something that involves giving.

That is the ultimate cure for despair and depression.
That is what we are here for.
That is why I'll continue to speak.

I don't know what caused the death of Robert Dziekanski. It may have been pre-existing conditions. The Taser application may have contributed. The physical nature of our confrontation may have contributed. The answer will always depend on who you ask.

I do know this. That wherever he is, his spirit still exists. I believe I have a debt to honour it. Through service to others. Through giving. Through helping and living a life, and doing as much good as possible.

Through saving lives.

I believe speaking is one of the ways for me to do that.

THE ONE QUESTION THAT WILL CHANGE EVERYTHING

Personal accountability is a trait that is *sorely* missing in today's society. From blaming to finger pointing to the "affluenza defence," no one wants to take accountability

34

for anything. Watch for it. When something goes wrong in someone's life, ask them why it went wrong. They will give you a lengthy list of misery and misfortune. It will almost always be missing one ingredient: *themselves*. Have you heard these stories? Have you told one?

The most important question you can ask about anything in your life, especially when something goes wrong, is this: How did I contribute to this occurring?

The moment you ask yourself this question, *everything* changes in your life. The moment you take accountability for your life and all that happens to you, is the moment you "pass from childhood to adulthood" as Jim Rohn says.

The moment I decided that I contributed to my charges and conviction by becoming a police officer in the first place, I stopped blaming everyone else and complaining.

Are others occasionally responsible when something bad happens? Absolutely. However, looking in the mirror before jumping at anyone else will slow you down. It will give you power. The power to know that, since you have contributed in some way to where you are, you have accountability and you can take action to change your situation. Accountability *is* power. And it mushrooms to other areas of your life.

The moment that I decided that I was responsible for my failed first marriage was the moment I realized that, in order for commitment to last with my wife Cindy, I have to ask myself daily, "What am I doing to contribute to the health of our marriage?" As my good friend Gilbert says, "You are the captain of the team." He reminds me that in order to win, I have to wear the "C" on my jersey. More responsibility? Yes. More personal power? Absolutely.

The moment I decided that, regardless of other contributing factors, a man died at my hands, was the moment I realized *my* life is no longer my own. I have a duty in this life – a responsibility – to give to others. I have one job for the rest of my life: to add value to others' lives. I believe that I was led to Toastmasters for that reason. Words are like water: they can save lives, or take them.

My *words* given in interviews, statements and in court led to me being convicted of perjury. That charge led to depression, PTSD, and thoughts of ending my own life. Words are like water – they can save lives, or take them.

My *words* given in the gym as a personal trainer have caused people to take actions that have lowered blood pressure, led to weight loss, and ultimately saved lives. Words are like water: they can save lives, or take them.

Words from Les Brown caused me to believe in myself. *Words* that I've written on paper and given life to through speaking have made people think, take action, and change their lives. I'd like to think that someone, somewhere, will hear *my* words and it may save their life, just as someone's words saved mine. Words are like water: they can save lives, or take them.

When things go wrong, I still ask "How did I contribute to this?" But now I ask another question: "How can I make things better?" That second question will change your life just like the first. It will cause you to help others. It will lead to healing. It will lead to hope.

PARTING WORDS

To improve the quality of your life, you must improve the quality of your choices.

- Barbara De Angelis

Finding fault in yourself sounds like a sure-fire way *into* depression and self-loathing. However, it doesn't have to be.

Most people simply point out their faults, mistakes and missteps and stop there. That causes despair, and that is why depression is an epidemic. Accountability is the answer.

Accountability is not about finding fault with yourself. It's about owning yourself and your actions. It's the decision that, no matter what happens, you took a step *at some point* that led you to exactly where you are, and so *some* responsibility lies with you. It doesn't matter if the "Blame Balance" is 90/10 (90% them, 10% you), 50/50 or 10/90. All that you need to worry about is your side of the scale. Your actions. Your next step.

Life doesn't change with talk, it changes with task.

Here's your task (and mine too). Take accountability for your life. Ask yourself how you contributed to the situation you are in. You will likely find a time that you had a choice. A choice to take one road or the other. Understand that, and own it. But don't dwell on it. Because, even if you can't find that "fork in the road" moment, you still have the ultimate choice.

You can choose *today* to be different.
You can choose *today* to take action, add value, and be accountable.
You can choose from this day forward, to Rise.

YOUR 1% WORKSHEET – ACCOUNTABILITY

1.   Think of all of the situations in life where you blamed someone else or where someone else blamed you. Was it a past relationship? End of a friendship? Family dispute? (Look back to your Angle 1% Worksheet as well). List your "Blame Balance" beside each situation. For example, if you believe that it was 80% their fault, 20% yours, write 80/20. Just go with your honest feeling right now.

2.   Now look at each situation. Write down *all* of the ways you may have contributed to the end result. Really think here – try to come up with any possible reason that would lead you to raise your blame balance percentage.

3.   Looking at all your previous answers, ask yourself: "What could I have done differently that would have led to a more positive result?" Now this doesn't necessarily mean that the result would have been different. Maybe the relationship or friendship would still have ended. This is simply about acquiring an attitude of accountability.

Note: If you feel resistance inside of you to do this exercise, it means you need it that much more. Maybe I'm alone here, but I had trouble taking accountability for some situations in my life. Accountability requires you to leave anger and resentment behind.

4 APPEARANCE

When we take action, an invisible force gathers all around us, pulling in opportunities that align with our purpose, propelling us with momentum to our freedom.

- Brendon Burchard

EARLY DAYS ON THE STREET

There are two types of policing: reactive and proactive.

Reactive policing works like this: You receive a call from the dispatcher, and respond to what needs to be done. This can be anything from an assault, to a theft, to a kidnapping or home invasion. It has been said that policing is long periods of boredom interrupted by sheer moments of terror. Simply stated, reactive policing is when you wait for the call, and then react.

Proactive policing is what you do in the "down times." It is the boredom-filling activities that simultaneously contribute to a safer society. It is how many police officers go from good to great.

In proactive policing, you don't wait for something to happen; you look for the crimes that do not obviously present themselves. This is *not* creating crimes to get people into trouble. Too many officers have made this mistake. Proactive police officers are the ones who drive down the side streets and do foot patrols instead of sitting in coffee shops. Proactive police officers create projects in order to find new ways to catch criminals. Proactive police officers check beyond the obvious and use their "down time" on the job to fight crime.

In short, proactive policing is about *creating* opportunities as opposed to waiting for them.

Life works the same way.

CREATING OPPORTUNITIES

If opportunity doesn't knock, build a door.

- Milton Berle

Being charged in 2011 forced me – for the first time in years – to look at the possibility of having to find a new career. During my 2013 trial, I discovered Toastmasters, but I did not think of anything more beyond re-capturing my confidence.

However, by 2015, I had mentored several other speakers, read numerous books on the art of Public Speaking, and taken courses in order to get better at the craft. It was then that I realized that there may be another outlet for me. I started to look at the possibility of becoming a professional speaker and speaking coach. I don't know where this will lead and whether policing aligns with that, but I know that life is about change and learning. You have to become comfortable with the fact that life's roads are always under construction. Sometimes you have to take action to make opportunities appear, rather than sitting around waiting for them to happen.

I've learned that on life's highway, adversity has a tendency to create a lot of damaged roads.

APPEARANCE AND ADVERSITY

There are many ways that adversity can throw you off course. Adversity is inevitable; it's your actions that determine whether you overcome it or not. We are basically life magicians – we can choose to create or make our solutions appear to us.

For example, when you face the adversity of hunger, you *create* a meal to get over it. When you face the adversity of not having the body that you want, you *create* a physical activity and nutrition program for yourself. (Or, you get someone else to create the meal or create the program.) For almost every adversity that you face in life, *you* can create your solution.

Let's look at three ways that adversity can be managed through solutions that *you* make appear.

CUSTOMIZATION

School is a rite of passage for most of us. We are placed in the school system before we can make many real decisions in life. School can be very good – we socialize, learn, and adjust to various forms of adversity.

We are taught to go to school, progress through the system, maybe even go on to post-secondary schooling through college or university. The next "logical" step is to get a job, get married, have kids, buy a house, and ride out anywhere from one to five careers until we retire on a modest income. There is nothing wrong with that path if that is truly what you want.

"Success is the progressive realization of a worthwhile dream or goal," Earl Nightingale said. If you are progressing toward what *you* want in life, then you are a success. If the aforementioned path is what you are doing and you are happy on that path, then keep going.

However, there are indications that many people are not where they want to be in life. Worse, most are not even taking any action that would get them where they would like to be. Be careful though: the people who are not advancing toward the life they want will not tell you that point-blank. It comes out in other ways, such as when they use clichéd statements that sound rational.

Here is what you may have heard.

➢ When you ask, "How's work?" you hear "Pretty good." or "You know, same ol', same ol'."
➢ When you ask "What's new?" you hear "Nothing much."
➢ When you ask "How's life?" they talk about anything other than how *their own* life is going. They will tell you that their spouse is doing well (hopefully), something about their parents, or most popularly, something new about their children.

Once again, if someone is doing exactly what they want to do, you *may* hear some of these answers. I challenge you to ask some more probing ones, however, to really test for truly personal customization of their own desired lives. Maybe even ask yourself some of the same ones.

Test Question: "What excites you about your work/business/career right now?"

Test Question: "Where do you see yourself a year from now?"

Test Question: "When is the last time that you tried something that scared you or that you were not sure of?"

If we are not careful, our lives become customized for us – and not in the ways we would like. Life is like the swimming pool: you don't want to just fall in, you want to plan your jump. Sometimes adversity can do that for us.

Look at your life, your failures, your challenges. Perhaps life is trying to nudge you into a change. Is there something in your routine that needs changing? Do you need to try something new? Is there a chance to customize your life differently?

My life was headed on a certain path before the events of 2007, and a change was required. However, it wasn't until I was charged in 2011 that I started to look at ways to customize a new life. I've learned a valuable lesson through all of this: Sometimes you don't know a customization change is needed, until something forces your hand.

Are there any signs in your life that you need to customize a new one?

COERCION

Facing judgement and ridicule "coerced" me not only to make a change in my policing career, but also in my life.

Many people have apprehension about consulting a psychologist. I must admit that at one time, I did as well. Many men seem to think they don't need help ("I don't need directions!"). On top of that, police officers, with

"Type A" personalities, often treat problems with the "brush it off and get back to work" attitude. However, as Barbara De Angelis, author of Soul Shifts states, emotions are like playing a game of "Whack-A-Mole." What you suppress in one area will pop up somewhere else. The point is that you may as well deal with the emotions directly because suppressing them leads to problems.

I walked into an airport on October 14, 2007. I took actions and a man died. A human being lost his life on my watch. Right in front of me. I watched a life end.

Less than a week later, I was back to work. No discussions. No psychological assessment. No processing. Just back to the beat.

I worked right up until the inquiry that began in January 2009. I testified in March of the same year. I walked into my psychologist's office one month later. Looking back, I realize that I didn't think I really needed a lot of help. But when I looked at the last few years of my life up to that point I said "Hey, maybe it might be a good idea to talk to a professional about this." I didn't think that I had any mental issues, but all of the negative press, disparaging comments, and hateful emails had finally gotten to me.

They say the greatest trick the devil played was convincing the world that he doesn't exist. Ignorance, contrary to the cliché, is *not* bliss. The only thing worse than having mental issues or illness, is *not* knowing that you have mental issues.

Life will send you lessons in many ways. Adversity is typically how many of us will be coerced into learning those lessons. And trust me, listening for the clues and learning the lessons is much easier than ignoring them, because when you don't listen, problems will keep popping up until you do.

But I am stubborn.

I had my first appointment with a psychologist in April 2009. Yet it took more than a year before she finally started to crack my shell. More than a year before the depression and PTSD were able to be uncovered. It was only after being charged with perjury in 2011 that I started to really look at my past, and its relation to my present. It was only after travelling back and forth to Vancouver for court, and being convicted, that I finally accepted what I believe has always been my life's obligation: to give to others, share my story, and help them heal through sharing theirs.

Adversity can be a random negative event – or it can coerce you to grow. The choice is yours.

CREATION

In 2007, I separated from my first wife. (Yes, 2007 was not the greatest year.) At the time, I was good friends with a fellow officer, and my wife was friends with his girlfriend. They planned a destination wedding, and it was time to send out invitations.

My wife at the time received an invitation. I did not. The choice of invitee did not bother me at all. What bothered me was the lack of a heads-up. The absence of a phone call from my friend, a fellow police brother. I thought we were closer. I thought I would receive a simple phone call explaining the reason – something like "I didn't want it to be awkward, so we went with her.." But...nothing.

Oh those life lessons. Sometimes you will get

reminders of truths that you already know. That day's reminder? That there are times in your life when people will choose easy avoidance over an honest conversation.

I'm not throwing stones. I've done it too.

But it bothered me. Later, when I told a friend about it, he asked me the simplest of questions. He said, "Have you ever asked him *why* he never said anything?"

Brilliant.

An obvious thing, yet I had not done it. Often in life we wait for situations to arise. We hold out for opportunities to come knocking. And many people die waiting for those opportunities. The truth is this: those opportunities will not always come to you. Sometimes you have to create the situations that will allow those opportunities to appear.

The simple end to that story...I called my friend, and we talked. I simply asked him why he never mentioned it. The reason – one I already suspected – was that he felt it was a bit awkward to start that conversation. Isn't it funny that we know many of the answers in life, but still want to hear them given to us?

THAT MALE MENTOR THING

My father died in 1996. He left when I was five, and was sporadically in my life until his death when I was twenty years old. He was a part of my life in a much bigger way than most absentee fathers, but still not in the way that a son really needs.

I believe a boy needs his father, and a girl needs her mother. No replacements quite do the full justice. A boy can learn a lot from his mother (and I definitely have) and a girl from her father. However, the same-sex parental relationship is irreplaceable.

I used to be jealous of the relationship that my friend Ian had with his father. He coached his soccer games, helped him with his homework, and taught him how to drive and barbecue. I'm not sure what void was left unfilled by my father, but I know I *did* feel the void.

I felt the void when I used to hide in junior school when the school bell rang at the end of the day. Every day I hid in the hallway, praying that my tormentor Bobby would skip his regular taunting and pushing and terrorizing. I felt the void when one day I thought I would outsmart him and ride my bike to school instead. "I'll just ride quickly past him and get home safely," I thought. He threw a rock with alarming accuracy and knocked me clean off my bike. It was the perfect getaway that never was. Oh, I felt the void then. I felt the void when I was bullied, when I had a crush on a girl, and when I was thinking I might want to try a sport. These are "man moments" when the void of being father-less is felt.

When you're missing something in life, the damage from its absence is magnified when you don't realize the problem. Sure, I remembered the feeling of missing a father, but in my adult years, I figured "My mom is a great role model, so she's all I need." She was (and is) an outstanding parent – but I made a lot of mistakes that may have been avoided had I realized that I needed some strong male mentorship. And most of those mistakes involved women.

My mother was (and is) a strong-willed woman. Looking back, I realize that I conceded a lot in my romantic relationships because I conceded even more to my mother growing up. Not speaking up can cost you. It cost me a lot of time and money. More importantly, however, I caused a lot of pain to the women that I had been involved with, simply because I did not speak up early or often enough. Sadly, it wasn't until my mid-30s that I realized that I needed some mentors.

I needed to learn the simple things. Respect. Honesty. Courage.

I'm still learning, but at least I've found some. Not in the conventional way, however.

My mentors come from books and audiotapes. I learn how to live from my *online* male mentors. Les Brown, Tony Robbins, Brendon Burchard, Jim Rohn, TD Jakes, and many more.

What you can't find, you must create. And when you create, you become what *you* needed for someone else.

That is the lesson of creation.

KEY QUESTIONS TO ASK

Your life is all about the lessons you learn, the love you give, and the legacy you plan to leave. Ask yourself these questions.
1. What are the main challenges in my life?
2. What have I done to create their appearance?
3. What can I do to create a solution? Can I customize a solution? Am I being coerced to a possible solution?

Brendon Burchard says that most of our solutions only appear to us *after* we take action. What can *you* do differently, starting now?

YOUR 1% WORKSHEET – APPEARANCE

1.   What does success mean to *you?*
Detail your response.

2.   Is what you are doing now
contributing to your definition of success?
If not, what can you do to create a more
successful future in your eyes?

3.   Are there roadblocks, personally or
professionally, in your life that you can work to remove
through trying something new? Look at your struggles
from a different vantage point, or better yet, ask a trusted
friend or mentor what they think.

Kwesi Millington

5 ACTION

It is vain that we talk of being men, if we do not the work of men.

- Frederick Douglass

WATER WISDOM

What's your sign? My answer to the cheesy pick-up line is a Cancer. I'm a water sign – as the horoscope goes – and that may be why I love the water. I could sit by the ocean all day. Perhaps people of all signs love this; I'm not sure. Nevertheless, water gives me peace. And wisdom.

Water keeps flowing, keeps moving. Even when it appears still, it is moving. And so are we. Your body looks solid, but it is actually a collection of trillions of cells, bunched tightly together, appearing "solid." That's the myth, that we are solid. We are actually a bunch of "moving molecules" propelled in harmony by our soul and spirit for a few decades of use. Even when you are "lazing on the 'La-Z-Boy'," your body's cells are always in motion.

Action creates life. Action sustains life. Action helps you to overcome adversity.

Action saved my life.

THE PILLS

I can remember contemplating suicide.

I can remember thinking the question. I had powerful pain killers. I had the equally effective sleeping pills. I sat on the edge of my bed, looking at the pills in my hand, asking myself one question: "How many of these do I need to take? How many – so I just don't have to wake up anymore."

The year was 2011. I had been charged a few months earlier with perjury. For the first time in my policing career, I really felt that it was over. I didn't know what to do with my life. Was policing just a job? No. For years it was how I identified myself. How I saw myself. Who I was. If I could no longer be a police officer, what else would I do?

The real question was: "Who am I *really?*"

Marianne Williamson, author of the book *A Return to Love*, states that "taking responsibility for our lives means taking responsibility for our thoughts." My thoughts were swirling in negative. The average person thinks over 50,000 thoughts per day, and many of those are repeated thoughts. All that I could think as I sat at the edge of the bed was that I had no worth. At that moment, no job and no career meant no personal worth. And since I had no personal worth, I believed that I had no reason to live.

I could not have been more wrong.

What you do is not who you are. What you cannot do does not determine who you are, either. I don't know if it was intuition, the voice of God, or just a hunch – but I had a thought that prevented me from taking those pills. What was the thought?

"Who needs me?"

I thought about my mother and the rest of my family. I thought about the friends who might miss me. It was then I realized that your life's worth is not who you are, but who you are to other people. The more that you do for others, the more worthy you will feel of the life you have been given. This realization has changed my life. I then evoked a previous step – Appearance – by asking one question: "How can I do more for others?"

The answer came to me as quickly as I asked it: Find a gym.

AND...ACTION!

I walked into the health centre unsure if they needed anyone. I dusted off my old personal trainer's certification and walked into the gym.

I had only one client that first month. But *one* was all that I needed.

I needed only *one* person to help.
I needed only *one* life to change.
I needed only *one* reason to start looking for more.

When I was charged with perjury, I forgot my value. Isn't it funny that we often define our *entire* worth based on one aspect of our lives: what we do for a living. You are so much more than the job that you do. I had forgotten that.

The US Bureau of Labor Statistics found that individuals between the ages of 18 and 38 will hold more than 10 jobs. Statistically speaking, I was due for a career change. I ought to have remembered that I once wanted to be a doctor, studied to be an accountant, settled on IT and Finance for my Bachelor of Commerce degree, got my Personal Training Certification, only to become a Police Officer in 2005. Life is about change. Sometimes we create that change; sometimes it is handed to us in the form of adversity.

THE FIRST MOVE

The most successful person is the one who can enjoy the scenery on a detour.

- W. Mitchell

The key is to keep driving, even when you are forced off the highway.

Jumping back into the personal training arena saved my life. It refocused me on what is important: adding value to others. That simple action forced me to take my eyes off of myself. You can only consider suicide when you're looking in the mirror instead of out of the window. The minute I got outside and started to help others – even in a small way – I forgot about my own problems.

That antidote for depression has always been my panacea. If you suffer from depression, let it be yours.

WATER MUST CONTINUE TO FLOW

It turns out that happiness that is true and lasting is quite simply this: progress. Progress = Happiness!

- Tony Robbins

"Enjoy the journey, not the destination." You have likely heard that before. You likely know that you won't enjoy "there" unless you are *fully* "there." So what happens when you finally get "there"?

Find what I call the trickiest of balances – the "calm climb": keep enjoying "here" while you set a new "there." Look for new mountains to climb while enjoying every step. Happiness is finding the delicate mix of presence and planning.

I have been in the fitness industry since 2001. In 2010, I competed in my first fitness model competition.

If you are not familiar with fitness competitions, imagine this. You work out 1-2 times per day, for 5 days a week, for 16-20 weeks (4-5 months). You eat a certain amount of carbohydrates, fats and proteins *every* day for that time, and your body gets more aesthetically pleasing week to week. You are excited and totally inspired by your change. You work tirelessly in the background, to finally get a chance to show off under the spotlight. The week before competition, you start to get even stricter with your diet, further manipulating sodium, carbohydrate and water intake so that your body "peaks" when you hit the stage. (Peaking simply means that your body looks as good as possible on show day. Remember this – the magazine models *only* look their *very* best for a few hours on *one* day!). You strut your stuff on stage...

Then it's over. You enjoy a night of "un-tracked" eating. Then it's back to...what? Just regular working out?

I entered a period of "fitness funk."

Have you ever heard of that? Fitness funk is the depression that hits a competitor after competing. The emotional low that strikes when the stage lights go out. I knew about it, but didn't give it much thought. Until I finished my first competition.

When I stepped off the stage, I no longer had any goals. I no longer had the drive to do anything more. I spent days flopped down on my couch, binge-watching TV, stopping only to get another bag of potato chips. I felt down and depressed. I didn't know what to do next. How did I get out of it?

I set a new goal.

Humans are goal-driven creatures. We need something to reach for. I moved on to other objectives and started striving for something new.

Water must continue to flow. Stale water collects bacteria and viruses. We are like water. Keep moving. Keep striving. Keep setting goals and flowing forward. That is what life is about.

In 2013, I found a new flow.

THE SECOND MOVE – PUBLIC SPEAKING

When I walked into that first Toastmasters' meeting with my enthusiastic friend Amparo, I did not know what I was getting into. I did not know where it would lead.

In the midst of my perjury trial, I thought "I need something to feel good about." I did not want to slip back into thoughts of depression. I needed to do something different. Something that would prove to me that I could do something positive other than policing. I was still helping a few people achieve their health and fitness goals. But I needed something more.

My psychologist has always advised that taking control of your life in the areas that you can control helps you to mentally manage your feelings about the areas that you can't control. I then heard the voice again: "Face your Fears."

I had a vague knowledge of what Toastmasters International was about. I knew that people joined to work on public speaking skills. What I did not know was how big the organization actually was. Toastmasters was founded in 1924 by Ralph Smedley to help people develop their communication and leadership skills. At the time of this writing, the organization has grown to over 345,000 members worldwide in 142 countries. In 2013, I joined one of Toastmasters' over 15,400 clubs.

Although my home club meets weekly (most clubs do), it took me four months to stand up in front of my fellow members to deliver my first prepared speech. I have to agree that public speaking is indeed one of the top fears that we face. However, it is a *learned* fear, not an innate one. As humans, we are only afraid of two things – the fear of falling, and the fear of a loud sound. All other fears – including the fear of public speaking – are acquired from our external influences. That being said, speaking still scared me. Yet I spoke anyways. And I eventually started to love speaking.

There is something to be said for facing your fears. Taking action in an area that you are unsure of makes you feel alive. It gives you energy. Facing your fears fills you with pride. I did not know that I would pursue professional speaking as a result of joining Toastmasters and delivering speeches. I just wanted something to feel good about. Something that I could point to and say, "Yes! I can accomplish something in my life again. I don't have to hang on to this feeling of worthlessness that my policing charge has created."

PARTING WORDS

It is not the critic who counts; not the man who points out how the strong man stumbles, or where the doer of deeds could have done them better. The credit belongs to the man who is actually in the arena, whose face is marred by dust and sweat and blood; who strives valiantly; who errs, who comes short again and again, because there is no effort without error and shortcoming; but who does actually strive to do the deeds; who knows great enthusiasms, the great devotions; who spends himself in a worthy cause; who at best knows in the end the triumph of high achievement, and who at the worst, if he fails, at least he fails while daring greatly, so that his place shall never be with those cold and timid souls who neither know victory nor defeat.

- Theodore Roosevelt

Action cures anxiety.
Action cures depression.
Action cures uncertainty.

There is nothing that happens in your life until you take action. I would have never re-discovered my passion for personal training, nor my love for the art of public speaking, without taking the first step. When you take action, you will find yourself. People often talk about "finding your passion." It can be difficult - even frustrating at times when you don't know what it could be. However, staying in constant action *will* get you closer to your life's mission. You'll never find your calling from your couch. Get out there.

Stay busy.
Start a hobby. Join a group. Learn a language. Take piano lessons.

Don't worry about finding a deeper meaning in everything. Just do something.

Next: understand your mind. In his book, *What to Say When You Talk to Your Self*, author Shad Helmstetter states that action is preceded by a feeling. That feeling is preceded by thoughts and beliefs, and those beliefs are preceded by the words that you say to yourself. In other words, your internal self-talk.

Don't think you talk to yourself? Try this: Sit quietly with a pen and paper, and write down all the thoughts that come into your mind. Thoughts such as "Why am I sitting here?", "What else could I be doing now?", "This is a silly exercise", or whatever you are thinking – this is all your internal self-talk. By verbally changing what you say, you program your mind, which creates new thoughts and beliefs, which lead to new feelings, and finally to new actions.

In order to take action in a direction where you have not been, start to write and speak new thoughts that will take you in that direction. Say things to yourself daily such as "I am an action taker," and "I am always taking action towards my goals and dreams," or whatever works for you. This will change your mind and make taking action an easier process. One final word on self-talk: it *must* be a daily, ongoing process.

If you're like me, at first you will think the process does not work. Keep going. Remember that your whole life up until now has been filled with self-talk in one direction. It's going to take a while to reverse that direction. But once you do, your life will never be the same!

Finally, action happens when you find a purpose greater than your pain. I'll repeat that: Find a purpose greater than your pain. Life will have its ups and downs. The question of pain is not of whether it will occur, but when. The only time that you will take consistent action is when you find a purpose – a reason that moves you from the inside. Find something that gets you going. Find a reason bigger than your fear. Bigger than your doubts. Bigger than your pain. That is the key to action.

If you don't have a reason that immediately comes to mind, find something or someone that you have an interest in. Do you have a spouse, parents or children that you can use as your purpose or reason? Do you have doubters in your life you want to disprove? People who are jealous of you, people who would love to see you fail? Use something you love – or something you hate – to drive you. However, remember that love is greater than hate. Even if the doubters or so-called "haters" motivate you in the beginning, finding a "love stimulator" will be a stronger fuel for you in the long run. Finding your path to purpose may be hard, but that will lead to your passion. Passion comes from the root word meaning "suffering." There may be some pain as you find your purpose and take consistent action towards your ultimate destiny, but your life will never be better than when you move.

YOUR 1% WORKSHEET – ACTION

1. Have you ever been stuck without knowing what to do next? In your life? In your relationship? In other areas? Do two things now. First, write down the question that you need an answer to. Second, write down the phrase "The answer is on its way to me now.." Finally, repeat that phrase over and over again, at least three times daily, and write down the answers that come. Trust the process. The answer *will* come.

2. When is the last time that you tried something new? (And I don't just mean trying a new burrito.) Keep a journal of your "firsts." Aim to try something new at least every month. Keep track and look back 6 months from now at how much you have changed.

3. Develop at least 10 self-talk statements that describe actions that you want to take. For example, if you want to start a workout plan, you could write down "I am motivated daily to go for a run/workout. I get up daily with energy and drive to exercise." Once you write down your statements, put them in three places where you *cannot* miss reading them every day. What are some good areas? Your bathroom mirror, your fridge, your car dashboard, your office, etc. Remember that you think 50,000+ thoughts per day. It's going to take a lot of consistent self-talk to counteract that!.

Kwesi Millington

6 ACCEPTANCE

Instead of putting people in their place, put yourself in their place.
- John C. Maxwell

PERSPECTIVE

I once heard a story about two men who were out ice fishing. They poked holes in the ice, put cold worms on their hooks, and plunged them into the icy depths of the water. After hours of fishing, the men caught nothing. Bewildered and disappointed, they were ready to give up and call it a day. Then one of the men saw a boy not too far from them holding his fishing rod over his hole in the ice. Beside the boy was a bucket full of fish! Astonished, the men approached the boy and noticed that his mouth was full. One of the men said to the youngster, "When you have finished eating, and your mouth is empty, you must tell us: How did you catch all of those fish?" The boy emptied his mouth, and showed the men the contents – worms! He said to the men, "I'm not eating. I'm warming the worms because that's how the fish like them."

I like that story because it reminds me to maintain perspective. The boy looked at catching fish not from his perspective, but from that of the fish. He was successful because he was able to look at a different point of view. How often do we look at the point of view of others? Have you ever judged without considering the "other side"? Accepting that there are other ways to look at a challenge or issue opens your eyes to new possibilities. It allows you to be patient with others, knowing that there may be facts or opinions that they are using in their decision-making process that you might not be aware of. Perspective changes everything. Accepting that not everyone sees things the way that you do makes the journey of life and its inevitable struggles easier to deal with.

Perspective gives you patience. Perspective allows you to show unconditional love. Perspective allows you to accept more about life that you may not understand.

JUDGEMENT DAY

God grant me the Serenity to accept the things I cannot change, Courage to change the things I can, and the Wisdom to know the difference.

- The Serenity Prayer

On Friday, February 20, 2015, I walked into the courtroom, hoping for the best, but prepared for the worst. Over the course of the past year, I have felt the tension in the courtroom during my perjury trial. I have felt the sting of hatred from Dziekanski's mother. I have felt the words of accusation for months from the prosecuting lawyers. I have felt the pre-judging stares and comments from the presiding judge. I walked into that courtroom, having long felt that the judge made up his mind a long time ago. I hoped that I was wrong.

When he pronounced me guilty of perjury, I didn't know what to think at first. I felt overwhelmed by numbness. I asked myself "How did it come to this? How did I go from doing my job, being reassured that I acted by the book, cleared by three separate police forces of all wrongdoing, being cleared of criminal charges, testifying at an inquiry with the hope of setting the record straight...to this?"

In order to be found guilty of perjury, the judge did not have to decide whether there were reasonable grounds to believe that I was guilty of perjury. Instead, he had to believe that there was absolutely no doubt that I was guilty of the crime. In other words, if there was any doubt whatsoever that I was guilty of the crime, a verdict of not guilty should have been rendered. After months of testimony, witnesses and statements, doubt was all over that courtroom. Witness's accounts described everything from Dziekanski waving the stapler above his head, to him grabbing a knife, to numerous diverging statements as to when (and even if) the Taser application took Dziekanski to the ground. Mistakes were made, not only by the officers when giving their statements, but by almost every single witness that was present on the night of October 14, 2007. Doubt was all over that case. There was so much reasonable doubt that even newspaper reporters had to admit as much in their writing. Yet, still the verdict was pronounced: guilty.

THE TRUTH IS WHAT YOU BELIEVE

My father used to tell me: "The truth is what you believe." It took me a long time to understand the verity of that statement. I thought that truth was truth, and lies were lies. There may indeed be facts that few could argue against, but that doesn't mean we don't try. The truth of my father's quote is shown by the fact that people will argue in favour of a certain belief, despite evidence to the contrary. They will find reasons for it to be true, and invent "logic" to back up their claim. Your thoughts tend to become your reality.

I have always told the truth in my case. I never lied about anything. Looking at everything that happened, most people could see that, with all of the versions of what happened on the night of October 14, 2007, mistakes could have been made during police statements and interviews and that there would be no perfect recall of the events of the night. An objective observer can see that errors do not equal lies.

It is difficult to convince others to change their "truth" once they believe it. However, there is something that is even harder to accept – it's harder to accept new truths that result from old injustices.

THE HARDER TRUTH

Resentment is like drinking poison and then hoping it will kill your enemies.

- Nelson Mandela

When you have been wronged, do you hold on to it? Do you let the resentment eat you up like a poison? Can you let that person be, or do you spend hours, days, and weeks hoping they will fall?

You will be tested in life. Your main tests will come from the following three areas: The values that you profess; the values that have been violated; and what I call the "Universal Values." Let me explain each of these.

AREA 1: The Values You Profess

You have probably seen it before. Someone tells you that they have a certain value, but when you see them in action, they do not live their words. There is truth in the statement that people listen to what you say, but watch what you do. It is almost as if the universe is waiting for you to speak about what you believe in, only to send you a "pop quiz" on its application in your life. If you observe closely, you will notice that soon after you open your mouth, situations will appear to test the truth of your words. Be ready. Many fail the test. If you are going to talk about it, then be about it, too.

AREA 2: The Values that have been Violated

When I was charged with perjury, I started asking myself, "How could someone accuse me of lying? How could I have been charged with this?" It took me a while (*years* in fact), but eventually I started looking at all areas of my life, not just my policing career. Once again, it was as if a message was being sent to me asking, "Kwesi, are you being honest in *all* areas of your life? Sure you may be an honest cop, but are you 'committing perjury' in your personal life?"

I hate those "Bags of Bricks" questions! Those ones hit you hard because you know they are true. Those ones remind you that *you* have to change. Those ones you try sometimes to ignore. Have you been there? My honest answer to that question was that I was an honest cop, but not the most honest son, friend, or boyfriend. Universal changes create universal growth. Regardless of what was happening in my policing life, I finally realized that it was time for holistic change.

Here is an exercise to try. The next time that someone wrongs you in some way, ask yourself, "Am I doing something in *any* area of my life that may be doing the same thing to someone else?" The answer may not be obvious. However, if you look at your life as objectively as possible, you will often find that you may be doing the exact same thing to someone else, and that what is being "done to you" can serve as a reminder to "fix your leak" in another area of your life. Maybe you have been wronged in a romantic relationship; that will remind you to fix an area of your relationship with a parent or child. Maybe a boss is "power-tripping" and micro-managing at work; that will remind you that you need to create more of a democracy instead of a dictatorship in your own home.

The key here is to pay attention. Almost everything in life is there to teach you something.

AREA 3: Universal Values

Regardless of your beliefs, there are values and principles that most people can agree on. Almost everyone believes that you should not physically hurt other people deliberately. Almost everyone believes that you should not damage or destroy something that belongs to someone else without provocation. (You probably should not do it in any case, but for sake of argument we will leave revenge out of this discussion.) Most people believe in the Golden Rule, in loyalty, and that honesty is the best policy.

Sometimes you may simply be tested in general areas that would make you a better person overall. You will be presented, for example, with situations that will test your loyalty. You may be given an honesty test. You may have a choice to hurt or help someone else. Life is full of tests, and your response to them will either build you up or break you down as a person.

The tests are coming and will always appear. Accept this fact, and be ready.

The hardest truth to accept is that when bad things happen, you have to accept them. Feel what you need to feel. Scream if you need to. Allow your emotions to play out. Then accept it. And take the next step...

Search for your lesson. Here's the caveat: it may not be apparent immediately. You may have to live through your situation for longer than you want to before the lesson appears. You may have pain and frustration while you wait. But it's coming. Just keep believing that something noteworthy will come out of something notorious.

Life is a test. It's up to you whether you'll pass it.

YOUR 1% WORKSHEET – ACCEPTANCE

1.   Think of any resentment that you are still holding on to. Is there another way to look at the situation that may make it easier to accept what happened? Think of how you can put yourself in "their shoes." Write out the other person's viewpoint.

2.   Write down five "truths" that you believe without exception. You may list more, but pick the most important five.

3.   Now write the opposite view of each of the five "truths" you wrote above. Is there a part of this new view that you agree with? What aspects could you support? You don't have to change your views or values, but look at the "grey," not just the "black and white."

.

7 ACCESSIBILITY

Vulnerability is our most accurate measurement of courage.

- Brené Brown

THE PUPPY PRINCIPLE

Why do we love dogs? There are numerous reasons why many people do. For the purposes of this section, let's focus on one: the act of submission. Dogs communicate non-verbally, and they do it very well. Any dog owner will tell you that not only do their pets understand certain commands given to them, but they are great at telling their human counterparts exactly what they want and when.

One act in particular is common among our canine companions. When they want to show submission, they roll over and expose their bellies to their owners. Sometimes they just want a belly rub, yes, but the act itself is a sign of submission. It is your dog or puppy telling you, "I yield to you as my owner and master of this home." They do this effortlessly, and without hesitation.

We could learn a thing or two from our dogs. There is power in submission. Many times the very things that we think make us weak actually strengthen us. This is not about showing someone else that they are your master or owner. Submission in human relationships just means that we are willing to show the vulnerable side of ourselves to others. By rolling over, a dog is telling you, "Here is my belly – the weakest and most vulnerable part of my body. I trust you with it. I trust you not to hurt me when I expose myself to you." When you can do that with your innermost feelings, your personal stories and your flaws, fears and frustrations, you become stronger, not weaker.

What I call "the puppy principle" is simply this: Submission leads to Success.

I do understand, though – it is not always easy.

SHARING MY STORY

I've never considered going scuba diving. I know it's a hugely popular worldwide activity. I know how to swim. But honestly, I'm afraid of going into the depths of the ocean. Maybe I watch too many movies. I wonder, "What if I run out of oxygen way down there?" or "What about sharks and other hungry sea creatures?" Call me scared, but I don't see myself ever doing that.

However, I can imagine why people love it. I've seen the TV documentaries. The depths of the ocean are beautiful. You will never see the entire beauty of the ocean by staying at the surface. You have to go deep.

The same goes for us as people in this world. You have to go deep. We have such surface conversations these days. Sure, small talk is acceptable, but not at the expense of meaningful conversation. When you meet someone, sure you see them. But we never really see each other until we dare to go deep. You will catch people off-guard when you do this, because no one does it. It's almost as if we are all wearing armour when we meet someone for the first time. We have to display strength at *all* times, or others may strike us down with their "scrutiny swords." We live in a world where everyone thinks someone is out to get something from them. It's as if we think "I'll only share with you those things that you *can't* hurt me with." What a mistake.

When I was charged and convicted, I was in the midst of getting heavily involved with public speaking. I became a Certified Public Speaking Coach, and focused on the art of storytelling. A big believer in practicing what you preach, I started saying yes to *any* opportunity to speak for free. For *anyone*. When I spoke to groups, I shared stories from my life. All stories – except for the one that I was living. I did not want to talk about my fears and frustrations regarding my personal story of injustice. I did not want to share my feelings. I refused.

That all changed for me after I spoke to the wisest person that I know: my mother. I asked her what she told people regarding my case. What she said to me changed everything in my speaking journey from that day forward. We were sitting in the kitchen, and before taking a sip of her tea, she simply looked at me and said, "Kwes, I don't necessarily talk about your case to people, but I don't hide it either."

Have you ever received the perfect piece of advice right when you needed it? My mom had hit the nail on the head. She wasn't trying to call me out directly, but her words did the job anyways. By not sharing my story with others, I was hiding.

This was 2015. I was doing a lot of travelling, back and forth between Vancouver and Toronto. I divided my time between my policing case and the difficult trial in Vancouver, and developing myself as a speaker and storyteller back home in Toronto. Every speech I would write had great storytelling elements, yet no elements from my current story of prosecution. I know now that the reason that I would not share was because I was afraid. I was afraid of what people would think of me. I was afraid of letting people see who I really was and what I really felt.

Vitriolic voices of self-doubt echoed in my head.. "Kwesi, how dare you speak of conquering self-doubt when you don't even know where your life is going? You are being charged with lying...and *you* want people to believe that you speak the truth? No one wants to hear your story. They just want to talk about you behind your back. They looked up your whole story on the internet. They're going to judge you. They all think what the media thinks: that you tasered that poor man to death, and then lied about it! And *you* are going to try to be a motivational speaker? Shut all that down before you embarrass yourself. Speak if you want, but not about that if you want anyone to listen!"

That's a *lot* of noise to listen to when you're trying to focus on motivating others. After a while, you have to stop ignoring the voices of self-doubt. You have to acknowledge them. That conversation with my mother made me realize it was time.

It was time to start talking about my story, and be damned if they like me, damned if they don't.

So I did.

I started telling people my story – on- and off-stage. I started leading with my story, instead of hiding behind it. I started talking for myself, instead of letting the internet talk for me. I started telling people that I was anxious; that I had fears and frustrations and I was not sure what my future would hold.

And then the magic happened. Everywhere I went, people started coming up to me and telling me their stories. They started opening up their lives to me, a stranger to them! I had people in tears telling me their own stories of suffering. It was humbling to me that people would tell a person that they had just met thoughts and feelings that some had not even told their families. I was truly honoured. And for the first time, I no longer felt alone in the venues where I spoke.

Finally sharing my story taught me a powerful lesson. We all have fears and frustrations. We all have something in our lives that we fear being judged for. We all have situations that we have suffered through that we don't want to talk about.

But you have to. You know that thing you don't want to say? That place you don't want to go? That talk you don't want to have? That is the very one you need to say or go or have. The words you don't want to say will get in the way of your ultimate happiness if you never say them.

Remember this phrase: In our imperfections, we make the deepest connections.

Share your feelings. Share your thoughts. Share your world. With your family, your spouse, your friends. Adversity has a funny way of connecting us to each other. So don't be afraid. Share your story with the world.

VERSIONS OF "YOU"

We are drawn to people who are real. We live in a world where you are supposed to show everyone Version B of yourself, but keep Version A hidden. Version B is your "Best" look – the version that you have placed in your mind as the one that people want to see. The version that is going to get you the best job, the best boyfriend/girlfriend, the best spouse, the best set of friends. That's the version that may get you tons of followers, but *no* real friends. That's the version that you show outside, but feel relieved to put away when you get home. That's the version that requires effort.

It's too hard to be Version B. Try Version A.

Version A is your "Authentic" self. The you that wakes up with crust in your eyes in the morning. The you that may swear, may not always be the best parent, friend, or spouse, but still tries. The version of you that says "this is who I am, take it or leave it." The version of you that may not get the best job, but will get the best job *for you*. The one that will end up with the person that you're supposed to be with, instead of the person who likes the shadow version of you. When you realize, as speaker and author Lisa Nichols says, that you have nothing to "hide, defend or protect," life becomes so much better.

Maybe you feel like going through your life is like holding your breath underwater. If you are around people who make you feel like you have to try or put effort in, you have two choices: you can hold your breath forever as Version B, or breathe freely as Version A.

I can't hold my breath that long. I prefer oxygen.

How about you?

IT NEVER ENDS

Have you ever stood on a beach and looked out to the ocean? It seems to go on forever. It feels like it never ends.

The "Art of Accessibility" is the same. You will be tempted every day to go back to "Version B." The voices of self-doubt will try to prevent you from being authentic. Most people give into that voice, and so few people show their real selves to the world. I fall into that trap too at times. I have to talk to myself and ask "What am I really thinking? What do I really want to say? How do I really want to show up to the world?" There is a force out there trying to suppress the authentic you. But here's the key: the true you wants to be authentic. The true you wants to show your light to the world at all times.

Have you ever seen a shy person who suddenly becomes talkative and expressive when they drink alcohol? You think "Wow, where did that expressive person come from?" That's just the frustrated authentic self trying to come out. That's just a portion of the real person trying to come out. Watch for the voices of self-doubt that try to suppress "you."

LET YOUR LIGHT SHINE

You are the light of the world – like a city on a hilltop that cannot be hidden. No one lights a lamp and then puts it under a basket. Instead, a lamp is placed on a stand, where it gives light to everyone in the house. In the same way, let your light shine before others.

- Matthew 5:14-16

You only need two things: courage and practice. The courage to share your truest thoughts and feelings (while sober), and the determination to practice doing this as often as you can.

YOUR 1% WORKSHEET – ACCESSIBILITY

1.   Write down 5 to 10 words that describe you (or who you are trying to be). Are you loyal? Honest? Outgoing? Shy? Introverted? Write down as many as come to you. If your list hits 20+ words, that's fine too!

2.   Look at the words on your list. Think of 3 to 5 situations in your life where you did not live up to your self-describing words. Did you act differently from who you are? Why did you act that way? To impress someone? To get something? Remember, if you don't recognize your patterns, you can't release them. Gain awareness of when you have slipped from "Authentic" self to so-called "Best" self by writing down your answers.

3.   Look at your answers to Question 2. Take a small step to change the way you interact with the people that you have not been yourself with. Start being real with them. Journal their reaction. Is it what you expected? How do you feel now that you have been authentic with them?

4.   Consider joining a speaking group. You can visit Toastmasters.org to find your local club anywhere in the world, or you can join a meetup community (through Meetup.com) or church group that allows you to share your story. I believe the key to connection is sharing the stories that make us who we are. And by doing that, as Marianne Williamson says, you "unconsciously give other people permission to do the same." You will gain confidence and power by simply sharing your story with others.

8 AWARENESS

When you realize that every single thing you experience in life has some benefit to offer you, you'll discover that there is no longer anything to fight against or to be defensive about. Not only that, you will discover that people, situations, and resources are drawn to you in ways you could have never predicted. This is when life becomes magical.

- Janet Bray Attwood

AND THEN IT HAPPENED

When I finished the first draft of this book, I was filled with a mixed sense of relief. However, I was still uneasy because I was awaiting the conclusion of my perjury case.

Just to recap: Robert Dziekanski died in 2007. In 2009, the presiding judge wrote a report condemning our actions from that night. In May of 2011, I was shocked to learn that I was being charged with perjury. In 2015, I was convicted, and I went on to lose my provincial appeal. Facing a two-and-a-half-year jail sentence, I went all in for my last shot: the Supreme Court Appeal.

From all that had gone wrong, I did not have high hopes. However, in May of 2017, I was granted a Supreme Court Appeal. I was surprised, to say the least. More than that: I became hopeful.

Just to get a hearing felt like a huge victory for me because until that decision, I had lost in every court proceeding that I had been a part of.

On October 30, 2017, with a new lawyer, and hopeful for vindication, I walked into the Supreme Court of Canada in Ottawa. There were basically three options on the table: a complete acquittal, an order for a new trial, or an upholding of the verdict. The Supreme Court looks at very few cases, and I came to understand that when they do take one, that it's because there is something the judges see in their preliminary perusal of the case that could affect Canadians as a whole. In my case, two of the four officers were convicted, and two others acquitted on the same charge, and with very similar evidence. I was optimistic that I would at least be granted a new trial.

What I did not expect, was that seven judges would take less than an hour to uphold my conviction with a 6-1 decision. I was left wondering why they even took my case in the first place.

Walking out of the courtroom I was in shock. Yes, I had lost the appeal, but after all I had been through over the past decade, I had become somewhat emotionally insulated from the worst-case scenario for a long time. However, losing that decidedly – and that quickly – made me numb. As I sat in my rental car for the long drive back to Toronto, I had so much to do... and less than 24 hours in which to do it. Fortunately, my good friend did the driving while I hustled to tie up loose ends such as cancelling my car insurance and gym membership. I couldn't process larger questions such as "How am I going to pay my mortgage from prison?" so I tackled the easy tasks. As I looked at the tear-stained face of my wife beside me, I don't remember saying much. The strongest sentiments need no words.

The next morning, after racing through the five stages of grief (denial, anger, bargaining, depression, acceptance), I turned myself in to the Maplehurst Correctional Institution in Milton, a city northwest of Toronto. Walking into an actual jail to start a multi-year sentence felt like a nightmare, and the fact that it commenced on Halloween was not lost on me. I thought that going to jail was the end of the road as far as what this whole case and past decade would teach me. Fortunately, I was very wrong.

THE FIRST WEEK

There have been two times in my life that I've had thoughts about suicide. The first was in the summer of 2011 after I was charged with perjury (see step #3 – Accountability). The second was during my third day in jail. Due to my history as a police officer, I was placed in solitary confinement to ensure my safety. After only 72 hours in solitary, I felt completely spent. After all, it wasn't just 72 hours...it had been ten years and 72 hours. I wouldn't say that it was the most severe suicidal thoughts you could have. I didn't think of how I would take my own life – I simply thought "I don't want to be here anymore." "Here," by the way, was anywhere at all.

From 9 AM on Tuesday, October 31, 2017, to the evening of Thursday, November 2 – a total of only three days—my mind jumped everywhere. For the past decade, I've had the threat of criminal charges hanging over my head, and for the past six years the possibility of imprisonment has been very real.

However, despite the odds, I still hung on to hope. Hope that my country's justice system would pull through. Hope that my innocence would eventually win out. Hope that my life could continue and that I could put this decade behind me.

But by a vote of 6-1 from the judges in the Supreme Court of Canada, it wasn't meant to be. And so I found myself sitting on a concrete bed in a windowless cell in Milton, Ontario, wanting to die. I was stuck in the past and despondent about the future. A short visit from my wife and mother on that Thursday evening was the only bright spot of that day.

Of course it was only a 20-minute timed visit – with a glass partition separating us. But I was willing to take that small solace. I could see their warm and loving faces, and through the visiting room phone I could hear the concern in their voices. I could be vulnerable and cry in front of them, and I could feel their compassion through the cold, thick glass. And then it was back to the cell.

I firmly believe that we are sent signs throughout our life that point us in the right direction. The only caveat is that we have to be attentive so that we don't miss them. On that Friday, fortunately, I was transferred to the Joyceville Assessment Unit in Kingston (the in-between jail for inmates while they await their final destination for "doing their time"). I say fortunately because, although I was still in solitary, I immediately received something that changed my perspective: a window. A dirty reinforced-glass pane, about the size of a basement window. Spend 72 continuous hours in a windowless room, and sunlight will feel like a hug from God. That instant positive feeling was multiplied when the guards allowed me to peruse the books in the prison library.

Then I saw the sign I didn't know I was waiting for.

WHAT'S WRONG NOW?

A few years before I was sent to jail, I'd read the book *The Power of Now* by Eckhart Tolle. To be honest, it was a tough read because some of the concepts were too esoteric for me. On the second read, however, I suppose I was more prepared for the words, and I enjoyed it. I think we see things with different eyes as we evolve. In the prison library, I simply started my search with authors that I was familiar with. And on the second shelf, I spotted another book by Tolle entitled *A New Earth*. Five hours later, I had completed more than half the book, and the reasons for my desperate depression of 24 hours earlier became crystal clear.

In the book, Tolle showed me that I had been thinking with my ego. The ego, as he describes it, is the "unobserved mind." In my case, that unobserved mind had taken complete control of my feelings. Our feelings manifest directly from our thoughts, and those thoughts will almost always be focused on either past experiences or future ideas, concerns, or predictions. In that mad scramble in the mind, we often lose sight of where our focus should be: on the present moment. That is what I had been missing – the main lesson that I had been missing – the last "A" – awareness of the *now*.

Tolle states that "the present moment is the field on which the game of life happens. It cannot happen anywhere else." The present moment is all that we have. The ego inside of us is what tries to focus on the "what has happened" and the "what will occur" thoughts about life. Those thoughts were driving me insane. They were causing my despair. They were keeping me stuck in sadness. It was only when I took Tolle's advice to stay in the awareness of the present, and what was good or bad about that very moment, that my thinking started to become a servant to my awareness.

I started by slowing down, concentrating on my breathing, and focusing on the "Now" moments throughout my minutes and hours in solitary confinement. In those focused moments, I would put the past and future thoughts away on the back shelves of my mind, and ask inwardly, "What is lacking in my life in this very moment?" Invariably, the answer returned that although I didn't have my freedom, I did have the following: food, a bed, and most importantly, my health. By the time I finished the book the next day, I learned that alignment with the present moment is the key to truly living.

Prison offered me the gift of despair, which pushed me to the gift of present moment alignment. Not the way I would have preferred to learn that lesson, but, as transformational coach Lisa Nichols states, "some motivation comes wrapped in sandpaper."

Every day is not perfect, but every day does have perfect moments. Moments where you can find a reason to smile. Moments when you can believe that everything is as good as it can be. Moments where you can find blissful peace. What I gained in all those hours of solitude is a new goal: to find as many of those moments as possible throughout each day. You will never find peace by dwelling on the past and future. When feelings of turmoil start to grow, take a silent moment and ask yourself this question: "What's wrong in *this* moment?" It's in those moments – where you forget the past and future and focus on the "now" – that the "peace that passes all understanding" is found.

REDIRECTION, NOT REFUSAL

Another key lesson I needed to learn was that the things I thought I was losing were in actuality just paths I was leaving behind. I've learned that in life, you are never refused, but simply redirected.

When I was diagnosed with depression and PTSD in 2010, my psychologist told me that I had a great ability to manage the disorder. While many self-medicate with alcohol or drugs, or simply become reclusive, I instead stayed active with various pursuits. I definitely had some very low days, but I was able to counter-balance those by venturing into fitness competition and public speaking. I am aware that I managed better than most. The average person facing a criminal charge, unemployment, and prison, who also deals with depression and PTSD, rarely jumps into fitness competitions and onto stages to speak in front of hundreds of people. However, coping mechanisms that are positive should nonetheless be recognized for what they are: activities done to re-direct destructive emotions.

Walking into prison meant walking away from all those activities. I believe that part of the anguish that I felt for that first week in solitary was due to the loss of my PTSD coping strategies. As the reality of my situation sank in, and I had no outlet for my emotions, I rapidly sank even lower. Jail meant silence, inactivity, and it left me with nothing to reach for.

One of my coping activities in particular showed that I had my priorities out of focus. When I was taken into custody, I was one week away from competing in a speech contest. I was looking forward to presenting my humorous speech in front of a large crowd and hopefully being crowned a champion. As small as that dashed desire was, it still bothered me as I sat behind bars. I was so sure that I was meant to win that little plastic trophy, which was going to lead to even more opportunities to speak. As I look back now, I'm embarrassed that I gave it so much mental energy. Thankfully, my time "inside" has taught me not only to exist in the present moment, but to surrender. The most peaceful way to a powerful purpose is to surrender the search for it. Maturity comes when you allow yourself to be led to your purpose. Stop pushing and pressing your way to what you think it is. When you relax into following instead of forging and forcing a path, your spirit will lead you to the meaningful bread crumbs to follow. As I sat in my 7-by-12-foot cell, the words by author Elisabeth Kubler-Ross gave me great comfort: "You will always get what you need, even if it does not fit into your mental picture."

When you're willing to give up what you think you're supposed to do, in favour of whatever nudges you in the present, you will find that you feel more in alignment. You will feel an ease in what you do, as opposed to a struggle. That doesn't mean that everything will always be easy (you still have to stay aware), but it will feel "right and light." Look forward to a purpose for your life, set goals, but be open to what changes may be offered to you along the way. And on the path, remember that there is true joy sometimes in simply "being" instead of "doing."

RITUALS

After a month in solitary confinement, I was through with just "being." I had accepted the fact that "today" was all that I need concern myself with, but boredom was inevitable. Presence has its place, but so does routine. To cope with 23 hours a day in a cell, I began to section that day into chunks. And though I was given a small television after the first week, I've never been a big TV watcher. So my day became a marathon of sections. I didn't have a clock, so I timed the day by mealtimes and lighting. When the hallway lights came on, I learned that it was between 6 to 7 am. After some meditation, prayer and spiritual reading, the jail door slot for breakfast clanged open and then I was offered "yard time" and a shower. The "yard" was a concrete area measuring about 12 feet by 12 feet, caged in barbed wire fencing, with a view of the inside of the prison grounds. Although I was glad to be outdoors, the mornings were starting to get cold, and walking in a circle for an hour was brutally boring, so I passed on that option after about day 5. A hot shower was soon the only reason I left my cell during the morning.

To make it to lunch, I typically just read (thank God for the library!) until the guards offered me lunch, which I soon found out was around 10:30-11 AM. Sometimes I would nap before "dinner" at 2-3 PM (yes, it was that early!), but I tried not to because I wanted to be tired at nighttime. So my days became more reading, normally some television, interspersed with pockets of meditation. Sunset and the lights in the hallway notified me that another day was over. That's how my daily rituals were established.

Time in solitary was achingly lonely at times, especially since problems with my phone card enabled me to speak to my family only a couple of times in that first month. Reaching from past to future back to the present moment became essential to prevent insanity. There is a good reason that nurses and mental health professionals check in on the welfare of inmates in solitary confinement daily. After five days an assessment is conducted to attempt to re-integrate the inmate into general population. However, the daily rituals that I established to protect my mindset, including the 21 books I read in solitary, helped me to get through the roughest time of my life.

The quality of your life is not established by the big things you do. It's established by the small routines you engage in daily. The quality of your life is determined by the quality of your habits. Rituals got me through my time in solitary, the rest of my time in prison, and continue to ensure that I am successful in life.

What are your rituals?

THE PROBLEM WITH PEOPLE

By the time I was transferred to the minimum-security side of the Joyceville Institution in Kingston, Ontario, I had learned two things: First, spending time alone is not only possible and bearable, it is essential. And secondly, there are angelic people in your life who will step up and remind you that you're not alone at all. However, the downside to the second lesson is this: sometimes the people that you expect to be in the second category are noticeably absent.

You may have heard that in life, people will leave and let you down. You may have even experienced this with people you know. In minimum security, I was finally permitted to have visitors for timed segments on weekends. As my wife updated me from the "outside world" as to who was applying to visit, I had three simultaneous feelings: gratitude towards those who completed the application and were waiting to visit me; surprise toward those who stepped up unexpectedly; and disappointment toward those I thought would apply, but did not. Here's what the problem was: I had expectations towards others. Expectation always leads to frustration. The quickest path to ruining a relationship is to paste a "should" on someone else's behaviour. The moment I released others to be who they are and do what they want to, I was actually releasing myself.

The only problem with people is that we *think* there's a problem with people. I've learned that the problem is never with people; the problem is with perspective. When those who wanted to write me letters or visit did so, I was grateful. *Full stop.* No expectations. After all, nobody ever had an intention to ignore me. And if a feeling of disappointment or judgment surfaced, I simply turned my thoughts inward and promised myself that going forward, I would become whatever I wanted anyone else to be. If I wanted someone to reach out to me, I decided I would start reaching out to them. If I wanted more kindness, I would start being more kind – starting with my fellow inmates in jail. If I wanted more attention, I would give more attention to those around me. I would "be the change" as Gandhi stated. And it started just a few days into my time in my new minimum-security home.

ALWAYS ADD VALUE

Strive not to be a success, but rather to be of value.

- Albert Einstein

A few days after I arrived in the minimum-security unit, I was told that I had to get a job. Everything from working around the grounds to working the library desk was available. However, I was fortunate that a tutoring job had just opened up. Most prison inmates do not have much of an education. As a university graduate, I had the opportunity to assist the school English teacher in tutoring inmates and helping them to earn their High School Diploma. Prison days often felt three times as long as those spent in freedom, so taking the tutoring job was a no-brainer to me. I actually found it crazy that some inmates chose not to work and spend their days with nothing to do but sleep, wander and think. Prison is really just a microcosm of the outside world: some choose to do something productive; others let their circumstances make them bitter instead of better. I had my bitter moments, mind you, but I found a way to minimize those.

Spending my days helping the inmate students turned out to be very rewarding. Through reading their assignments, I learned many of their stories, and saw that many "criminals" were not bad people – they were just good people, who made one bad mistake. I stopped looking at myself as better than the rest of them because I was the innocent cop stuck with all of these bad people. I realized that I was no better than anyone in that jail. I just had different opportunities throughout my life, and had made choices based on those opportunities. When I started to look at myself as similar to those men instead of as someone special, I changed my mindset from "Should I help them?" to "HOW can I help them?"

I stopped judging, and I started to help. I stopped rendering mental verdicts, and I started adding value.

When your life is about adding value to others, you forget about yourself. In the moments when I was helping others, it became easier to forget the injustice of my incarceration. In life, I've learned that you stop your hurt when you help.

HALFWAY THERE

On May 1, 2018, I finished my six-month jail sentence, and moved into a halfway house in Hamilton. Although I was not totally free, I was basically so. I had to sleep in a house and report to staff four times per day, but I could use my phone, drive my car, and most importantly, go home and see my wife every day. I was told that there is a strange feeling that inmates get when they are released. I didn't think that I would fall victim to it, but I did. I call it "prisoner's remorse."

In the jail classroom, I'd see many inmates receive notice of their parole not with happiness, but with trepidation. You'd think "you're going to be released" would be great news for someone in jail to hear, but many inmates have gotten used to the prison routine. Sure, we were under the control of guards and on a constant timetable, but at least it was a consistent one.

When on the "inside," many don't think about family obligations, job interviews, or mortgages. They do what they can about those things before incarceration, then forget about them when they can no longer be in control. For many, freedom is akin to being dropped into a foreign country. Some have no home, no job, and no money. They may have been ordered around and treated poorly in prison, but they were also clothed and fed. They had a place to sleep and an order to their lives.

Freedom means a rush of uncertainty. Without a plan or support system, many experience a form of depression and yes, a hesitation about being paroled. There's a reason why approximately one in three adults re-offend. The numbers here in Ontario are improving, and halfway-house support systems help with that, but "prisoner's remorse" is real.

While I do not fit the "typical offender" profile, I experienced a different kind of gloom in my first few weeks of "halfway freedom." Meditation, awareness, and "practicing presence" had become the staples of my daily life in jail. However, once I was outside, the distraction of new lists, obligations, and general busy-ness became overwhelming and sent me jumping back into my past and future. While I was grateful to be finally free, I missed the short list of responsibilities I had left behind. Crazy! And that was just after spending *six months* in jail! I can't imagine someone who comes out after years inside.

Life teaches us lessons, and I've learned that no matter how proficient we become, we need to remind ourselves of them throughout our lives. For me, that meant simply returning over and over again to the present moment. The "now." The only place that I will ever be. The only time that I can ever affect. The only moment where I can feel peace. Sure, I planned future goals, imagined future dreams, and set future intentions. But I've learned that life is about striking the balance between pursuing the future, while enjoying the present.

The future is a fictional term. All that exists is "the present moment" to come. In those moments, the goal is simply to respond as guided. In their book (which I highly recommend reading and applying) The Passion Test, authors Janet Bray Attwood and Chris Attwood outline a simple truth: "When the mind is calm, then inspiration is natural." The key to tomorrow is mastering today. And mastering today starts with the peace that exists when you align yourself with the present moment – the now.

WHERE ARE YOU GOING?

On August 30, 2018, I left the halfway house for the last time. The journey that started almost twelve years earlier at an airport in Vancouver ended with an anti-climactic walk out of my temporary home in Hamilton. I was going home – this time for good. But more importantly, I knew where I was going in life.

As I write these words, I don't know what challenges lie ahead, but I do know the theme of the journey. In my early years as a police officer before 2007, throughout the past decade of uncertainty, and right up to the present moment, there has been one constant theme. The one area where my passion has never waned has been my fervent desire to mentor and motivate youth.

Suicide is one of the leading causes of death among the young. I see rampant low self-esteem, exacerbated by peer pressure, bullying, and social media. I see widespread apathy and false entitlement. The more I see, the more my desire to help has multiplied. I've turned my speaking skills towards youth empowerment, and my mission is to teach them that challenges are meant to build you, not break you. I want them to know that while there is peace in being in the present, the "now" will be replaced tomorrow by an even greater "now," and what feels like forever is just a moment that will pass. And I want them to remember that it's the character they build through crisis that counts. Anyone can smile when the sun is shining.

Where are *you* going in life?

Prison taught me that the exact details of what you will do are not important – it's the direction that you want to go that will illumine the path you need to follow. I knew I wanted to help fellow inmates. Once I made that decision, the means of becoming an English tutor was shown to me. Identify the way you want to live, stick to that decision in faith, and your path will be shown to you.

YOUR 1% WORKSHEET - AWARENESS

1. Think back to the last time that you were upset. Ask yourself what you were thinking in that moment. Did your concern have to do with something related to the past? Or, was your worry related to the future?  Chances are what concerned you was related to yesterday or tomorrow. The next time you are upset, ask yourself this "If there was no yesterday, and no tomorrow, would I truly be upset right *now*?"

2. Develop a "Presence Practice." It doesn't have to be meditation, but something as simple as taking five conscious deep breaths daily, in complete quiet, with no distraction will suffice. Count your breaths in and out slowly, counting each second it takes to inhale and exhale (1, 2, 3...on the in-breath and out-breath). You may notice that your mind wants to stray even from this. Don't worry if it does; just make it a daily habit to do the five breaths in silence. Build up to ten breaths when you are ready.

3. Look at the activities and projects that you are working on. Are you trying to fit what you want into something that's not for you? Are you doing things because everyone else is doing them or because you think that is what you're supposed to do? A good hint that you may be pushing towards a goal that isn't meant for you is that you keep running into inner resistance and a lack of enthusiasm or joy when you keep trying to move in that direction. Ask yourself if you really need to be

doing everything, or if some activity you call a "goal" is draining your inner peace.

4.   Think about the last time you were angry with someone. Were you angry at them for something they "should" or "should not" do? Anger towards others often comes from expectations. Release the need for anyone to conform to your blueprint for how they "should" act. Watch for these opinions the next time you are tempted to get mad at someone who doesn't act the way you expect.

5.   Find a way to help someone who can never pay you back. Do this tomorrow. Do it often. Volunteer your time. Give money to a homeless person. Donate $1 when the cashier at the grocery store asks: "Would you like to give $1 to _____?" Find a way to help others and expect nothing in return as often as you can. Your path to joy lies in philanthropy – not just in giving of time and money, but of love.

Kwesi Millington

BEGINNING

Most people call the end of their books the "Conclusion" or "End of the Journey." I prefer to call this the Beginning. If you've picked up this book, it's likely because you're a friend that I've badgered (kidding!). Or you have pain in your past that you want to rise above. If you fit into the latter category, consider this a beginning.

Take each step and apply it in your life. Take the following main points to remember for each of the 8 Steps to Overcome Adversity.

Step 1: Association
The reason you are here, is because of what you did there. (It's all related)

Step 2: Angle
What you see is what you will be.

Step 3: Accountability
When seeking to blame, look in the mirror, not out the window.

Step 4: Appearance
If you can't find the door, build your own.

Step 5: Action
Your behaviour proves your belief.

Step 6: Acceptance
You can only change what you first allow to be.

Step 7: Accessibility
Share who you are with others, because it's in our imperfections that we make the deepest connections.

Step 8: Awareness
Your future path is paved by presence.

START FROM TODAY

Go forward today. Take what has happened to you and use it as fuel, instead of falling victim to fear or staying mired in frustration. Use the eight steps, and what resonates within the words that you have read. Then go a step further. Listen to your own interior voice. The answers for how to rise above adversity are, and always have been, inside of you. All that I can hope this book to be is a reminder of what you already know deep inside.

I hope our journey together has been beneficial to you.

You were meant to rise. I like that...let's call ourselves "Generation Rise."

Go do it.

Namaste...
Kwesi

ACKNOWLEDGMENTS

I'm reminded of the point John Maxwell makes in his book, *Winning with People*. "When you look at your successes, you will always see people in the picture."

Simply sharing my story has taken a long time, and I realize that actually getting it out and putting it on paper for anyone to see is not something that I was able to do on my own. There are many contributors to this book, most of whom likely have no idea that they helped. I may not name them all, but I will try my best.

There were four of us on patrol that night at Vancouver International Airport. I could not have gotten through to where I am today without them. To Monty Robinson – you have always been a leader to me, from the streets in Richmond, to the night of October 14, 2007, and beyond. To Gerry Rundel – I still remember your gentle nature and thinking "Wow, this guy's a cop?" I know why you joined the force, and your strength in the continuing battle has been an inspiration. To Bill Bentley – what can I say? A truer friend in good times and bad, I could not have asked for.

To those of you who wrote me letters at my sentencing and reminded me what real friends and family can do for you – Agnes Graczyk, Alain Beauchamp, Alpha Snaggs, Amanda Sutherland, Amparo Cifuentes, Anna Denny, Benjamin Barkow, Brenda Marks, Brian Edwards, Colin Morgan, David Bellamy, Dr. Paul Wright, Ed Alvarez, Evena Patricia Gottschalk, Frank D'Urzo, Gilbert Thompson, Ian Marks, Ismay Bowles-Gabler, Jackson Bernard, James & Mary Anne Bennett, Jason Snaggs, Jeff Gleeson, Jennifer George, Johanna Mihailiuk-Geary, Karen White-Boswell, Karina Peterson, Kenny Cruickshank, Keri Johnston, Kike-Lola Odusanya, Kim Hawkins, Kojo Millington, Makayla Bentley, Megan Purton, Meghan Young, Melrose Cooley, Michelle Makowka-Skoko, Nelia Silva-Millington, Nia Millington, Paul Cooper, Paula Harris, Peter Henry, Peter Marks, Raphael Francis, Richard & Esther Marks, Roland & Sandra Wilson, Rosemary Rooke, Santy Yeh, Shane Parrott, Sharon Bone, Vance Morgan, Veronica Fox, Wendy McBurnie, Ying Fai Wu, and Yvonne Provost – thank you from the bottom of my heart. The sentencing may not have gone the way we had hoped, but your love was felt.

To my psychologist, Deborah Nixon. This book would not have happened without your constant support, and persistence to break through my stubbornness. It took almost a year for me to start really opening up to you, and you've guided me to understanding myself in a way that I did not even think possible. You are truly the best medical professional (along with my family doctor Dr. Sidenburg) that I have ever encountered. Thank you for sticking with me, and helping me to get out of my own way. I am truly blessed.

To Mike Ingles. I could not have gotten anywhere in this mess without you. From Day 1 you've been not only a support to me at work, but also a great friend. An extension goes to your former assistant, Sherrie Cohen. From booking my travel to making my countless trips to Vancouver that much easier, your support has been invaluable. Thank you both.

To Curt Petrovich. Thank you for keeping an open mind. Thank you for giving us a voice in a bigger way than we could have ourselves, and thank you for continuing to share our story, which in many ways is linked with yours.

To Helen Slinger. Thank you for bringing our story – even as a small part behind Curt's – to the country.

To Leo Knight. Thank you for being the bold voice of truth and your unending support of the four of us.

To Sarah Hilton and Jeremy Tracey. Your advice and words of wisdom in helping me give voice to my stories and speeches were a key part of building my courage to write this book. Thank you.

To my editor, Victoria Barclay. Thank you for taking the thoughts I have put on paper and helping me to make sense of them. Thank you for your time and wisdom in helping me put together this book.

Finally, as stated at the beginning of this book, my mother and my wife are my "female foundations." They are God's gift to me. My gift to Him is to speak, write, and give my all to them and the world around me every day.

Manufactured by Amazon.ca
Bolton, ON

31264407R00059